Leadership & Strategy Lessons
From Alexander The Great

LEADERSHIP & STRATEGY

LESSONS FROM

ALEXANDER THE GREAT

Traits, Behaviors, and Strategies of the Only Person
Who Conquered and Ruled the Known World

Leandro P. Martino

ISBN: 1-4196-8041-2

ISBN-13: 978-1419680410

To order additional copies, please contact us.

BookSurge Publishing

www.booksurge.com

1-866-308-6235

orders@booksurge.com

Printed in the United States of America

"TO THIS EMPIRE THERE WILL BE NO
BOUNDARIES BUT WHAT GOD HIMSELF HAS MADE
FOR THE WHOLE WORLD."
ALEXANDER (THE GREAT) III OF MACEDON

To my parents

CONTENTS

Chapter I

The Quintessential Leader

"There was at that time no race of mankind, no city, no single individual, to which the name of Alexander had not reached."[1]

Arrian (historian, second century A.D.)

STUDIED, COPIED, AND admired by leaders of all times—including Roman emperors, Napoleon, and modern leaders such as Ted Turner—worshipped as a god during his own life, Alexander the Great remains the best example of leadership, unmatched after more than 2,000 years. He was the most powerful person who ever lived and ruled the known world without limitations. He built incommensurable power gradually from a precarious base, and we remember him today as the finest conqueror and greatest military genius of all time.

Alexander lived thirty-three years, and he reigned for only twelve years and eight months; but he left a profound and lasting mark on the world. He founded and built dozens of cities, many of which still exist, and he caused others to disappear forever from the face of the earth. He founded the capital of ancient Egypt, Alexandria, considered the "New York" of the ancient world. Alexander produced a cultural exchange between the West and the East that changed the history of the world. His conquest contributed to shape the culture and the world, as we know it today.

His achievements were so marvelous that, almost 900 years after his death, the inhabitants of an oasis close to Siwah (Egypt) were still worshiping Alexander as a god, even though Christianity had been the official religion of their territory (Roman) for 200 years. Even the powerful Roman ruler Julius Caesar was daunted to learn that the Macedonian had conquered the known world—and at a very young age. He was so overwhelmed with frustration when he compared himself to Alexander that he broke down and wept before a statue of Alexander.[2] Besides Napoleon, Julius Caesar, and other Roman rulers, almost every major general in history looked up to Alexander.

Alexander possessed a relentless power of endurance and a sharp intellect, which was only surpassed by his courage. Educated by Aristotle, one of the most influential thinkers in the world, he became a warrior at the age of fourteen, a general at eighteen, a king at twenty, and the sovereign of most of mankind at twenty-five. In a fast-changing world, populated by billions of inhabitants, people often do not remember the leaders of five years ago.

Yet, numerous documentaries, movies, and history books still re-mind us of the *insane* goals that a young man from Macedonia* accomplished three centuries before Jesus was born. The former President of the University of California and professor of Cornell University, Benjamin Wheeler, wrote, "No single personality, ex-cepting the carpenter's son of Nazareth, has done so much to make the world of civilization we live in what it is as Alexander of Mace-don. He leveled the terrace upon which European history built."[3]

The purpose of this book is to analyze the traits, behavior, and strategies of the only person who successfully conquered and ruled the known world, to compare them with modern theories, and to show his similarities with other outstanding leaders.

Throughout history, the destiny of millions of people has de-pended on the qualities of their leaders. Many people have devot-ed a good part of their lives to lead their countries, communities, and organizations, but only a few of them have succeeded and emerged as remarkable leaders. Why is leadership so difficult? What did Alexander do differently from the rest? How did he achieve virtual worldwide success in only twelve years, without los-ing a single battle? These are just a few of the questions that this book will address.

Far from becoming obsolete, most of Alexander's traits have become increasingly important in our times. Leadership and strategy, which we cannot separate, are not only craved in the political and military arena, but they are also vital for prosperous

---

*Ancient kingdom (also called Macedon) in the northeastern part of ancient Greece.

companies and non-profit organizations. Furthermore, a healthy society depends on the quality of its leaders. While some wise leaders have earned praise for building empires, many incompetent ones should take the blame for the decay of the societies and businesses they have led.

The urgent need for such scarce, wise leaders is apparent in the disproportionate, increasing compensation of CEOs, and in the fierce competition to attract leaders and strategists at different levels of organizations.

It is not a coincidence that so many successful leaders of different times have studied Alexander's *secrets* and applied them to their ventures. By learning and mastering the outstanding traits and behaviors of this quintessential leader, they have gained precious, insightful knowledge to succeed in their respective arenas.

Alexander did not conquer the known world by chance, nor did he win every battle he fought by fortune. He had a method—a method that can be learned.

The Day the World Changed

The month of September was coming to an end in the year 331 B.C., and one of the most impressive battles in history, the Battle of Gaugamela, was about to begin.[†] King Darius III of Persia had chosen a flat ground for the battle to capitalize as much as possible on his great superiority in the number of soldiers. His im-

---

[†] This book does not follow a chronological order but rather uses a thematic approach to analyze Alexander's leadership and strategies. Readers will find a chronology at the end of the book.

pressive army was estimated as one million foot soldiers, 40,000 equestrians, 200 scythe-chariots, and some elephants, while Alexander's force consisted of only 7,000 cavalry and approximately 40,000 foot soldiers.[4] This represented more than twenty Persians per Macedonian, in a time of hand-to-hand battles.

Following a long journey and after receiving the information of Darius' position, Alexander stalled seven miles away from his enemy and remained there for four days to rest his soldiers, check horses, polish weapons, and plan for the battle. He left behind pack animals, baggage, and soldiers unsuited for war. He then resumed the march[‡] toward Darius, halting again about four miles away from the Persians the night of September 30. The Persians were already prevised and lined up for fight. Alexander then called for a meeting with his officers to decide on a plan of action. His alternatives were to fight Darius that same night, as the majority of his officers asked him to do, or to follow General Parmenio's advice and wait until the following day.

Alexander, together with his light infantry and the Companions, one of the finest and best-trained cavalry units in history, performed a careful inspection of the entire battlefield. Then he called a second meeting with his commanders and examined carefully the pros and cons of each alternative. This time the king decided to endorse Parmenio's suggestion.

These were the main points of Alexander's rationale for delaying the attack. First, by waiting until the following day, he could

---

[‡] Readers will find a map of Alexander's marches at the end of the book.

keep the Persians waiting another day and night under arms. Meanwhile, his soldiers would lay down their arms and stay rested for the battle.

This would not only have an impact on the soldiers' fatigue before the fight but would also test the nerves and morale of the Persians. Waiting for the night attack that would never materialize would stress the Persians. Second, waiting until the next day would give Alexander enough time for a minute inspection of the battlefield and the enemy's dispositions. Third, a night attack would be a risk. Even if Alexander won, the darkness would give Darius an excuse for his defeat. Finally, while the majority of his commanders wanted to advance at once and attack under cover of the darkness—because it would cause confusion—Alexander did not like the idea of "stealing victories like a thief."

From the top of a hill, he saw the overwhelming number of soldiers whom Darius had put into the field, already under arms and standing in battle order. He decided to halt and keep the gigantic Persian army waiting under arms for another day and night.

During said night, the Persians indeed kept ready for battle, fearing a nighttime attack. Hour after hour, they waited in arms, alert, with their lives at stake. The attack, however, did not materialize during the endless night of September 30 because Alexander had ordered his army to halt, lay down their weapons, refresh themselves, and rest. The last order he gave was probably the most difficult one, as his soldiers had already seen the approximately 100,000 campfires of their enemies, and such a large number of soldiers naturally disturbed them.

The following morning, his troops were understandably more invigorated than their counterparts, who had kept expecting, and stayed armed, stressed, and awake. He had minutely planned the disposition of his forces. On the right wing of his army, he positioned the Companions, led by the Royal Squadron under the command of Cleitus. Next to them and toward the center, Alexander placed squadrons under several officers. The shock infantry (phalanx) of the Guards was located next to the cavalry, and other Guard units led by Nicanor supported its left. Next to them, toward the left, were the units of Coenus, Perdicas, Meleager, Polysperchon, and Simmias. Craterus led the foot unit in the left wing and next to him were the allied cavalry squadrons, supported by the Thessalian cavalry. This last cavalry expanded toward the left wing of the ground forces. Parmenio (also Parmenion) led all the left wing.

Fig. 1. The Macedonian Phalanx was equipped with *sarissas* (long counter-weighted pikes)[5]. **Note**: all the illustrations and maps in this book are approximations.

Behind the front lines, Alexander located reserve troops to anticipate any attack from the rear and to protect the entire army. These troops had orders to watch for an encircling attack—very likely due to the Persians' heavy numerical superiority. In the case of such an event, the reserve troops had instructions to meet the endangered attack. In addition, Alexander reinforced both wings with backup troops, so they were ready for a swift defense in case of an encircling maneuver. On the right wing, half of the Agrianes led by Attalus and all of the Macedonian archers were placed forward at an oblique angle, ready to broaden or close the battlefront as needed. The mercenary cavalry, led by Menidas, was located right in the front line with instructions to turn and strike the Persians in the flank—if the latter attempted an encircling maneuver. On the left wing were the Thracians, led by Sitalces, at an angle with the main force and supported by cavalry. The over-all formation was so adaptable that the back troops could roll around the entire army and reach the front line in case of necessity.

Such was the level of detail and perfectionism with which Alexander planned his fights. He forecast his enemies' chess moves and planned the responses for each alternative as much as possible. His enemies usually surpassed him in numbers, but he would not allow them to be better prepared for a battle than he was. Alexander was brilliant at doing his homework and anticipating dangers.

A memorable battle, still studied after more than two millennia, was about to start on October 1. The fortune of an entire era was decided on that single day. We will come back to this battle towards the end of the book, after we analyze Alexander's unique qualities in the following chapters.

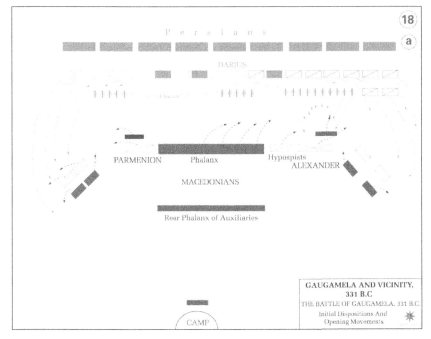

Fig. 2. Courtesy of the Department of History, United States Military Academy.
(Infantry: solid rectangles; cavalry: hollow rectangles)

Chapter II

The Speed Advantage

"A good plan violently executed now is better than a perfect plan executed next week." George S. Patton[1]

OVING FAST AND being early has numerous advantages, including the benefit of surprise and the possibility of finding one's adversary unprepared without the time to get organized. As professional chess players know well, the party who moves first has more chances to impose an opening that is convenient for the player, or inconvenient for his or her opponent, and so the first mover gets the upper hand. Nowadays, a leader's ability to act rapidly and steadily is, at the very least, as important as it was two millennia ago.

This chapter shows one of Alexander's trademarks: his proverbial speed of movement in reacting and responding to the challenges that fate presented to him. Whether at the beginning of his campaign, when he was only twenty, or as an experienced conqueror, Alexander was always one step ahead of his rivals—even surprising the men who fought by his side.

Alexander inherited a questionable and unstable power as king of the relatively small Macedonian territory* at the young age of twenty. It took him less than thirteen years to consolidate his inherited power and to conquer the known world as no one ever did before or after him.

Early in his campaigns, he acknowledged that he had several disadvantages in comparison to his major enemies. Therefore, he exploited his speed to compensate for his shortcomings.

Promptly Establishing a Power Base

Alexander was only twenty years old when his father, Philip II of Macedon, was murdered in August 336 B.C. Alexander did not have a mentor to guide him. Even though the loyal General Antipater recognized him as Philip's successor to the throne, General Attalus, a personal enemy of Alexander and his mother Olympia, decided to follow the orders of Prince Amyntas—former child-heir to the kingdom. Attalus represented a deadly threat to Alexander's aspirations. Attalus was then in Asia commanding half of the Macedonian troops.

---

*A region of the Balkan Peninsula in southeastern Europe that now comprises northeastern Greece, the southwestern corner of Bulgaria, and the former Yugoslav Republic of Macedonia.

Alexander's lack of experience did not prevent him from taking a bold action to hinder his enemies and start building his power base. When the news of Attalus' rebellion reached Pella, at that time the capital of Macedonia, Alexander made a fast decision: he would send an army to Asia. Hecataeus, one of his supporters, led the army with orders to arrest Attalus and bring him back to Pella, to face judgment and execution for insubordination. Hecataeus had an alternative: he could kill Attalus as soon as possible. History tells us that Hecataeus crossed into Asia and killed Attalus himself or had a third person kill Attalus when he resisted. Prince Amyntas managed to escape for a short time, but he was eventually arrested and killed as well.

Fig. 3. Contemporary image of Pella (ancient house atrium).[2]

Alexander's rapid and decisive action helped him to gain the respect and support of the Macedonian people, who had followed very closely the humiliations and challenges that he had to overcome. Alexander's speed established his legitimate power. Legitimate power is one of the five sources of power proposed as categories by French and Rave's research (1968)[3] in a widely used approach to sources of power.

Legitimate power is based on an individual's formal position in a group or organization. People comply with the leader due to belief in the legitimacy of the possessor of power. This source of power, together with reward and coercive powers, is known as a position power. It is vested in the individual, and that person has access to this power because of the position he or she has in the group or organization. Since the source of these three types of powers relates to the individual's rank, the most likely reactions from followers are compliance or resistance, instead of commitment and acceptance, as in the case of expert power and referent power.[4] Further discussion on power sources will appear in following chapters.

The Time Value

"There is one kind of robber," said Napoleon Bonaparte, "whom the law does not strike at, and who steals what is most precious to men: time."[5] Alexander was not as extreme in his statements, but he considered time a very scarce resource.

Many Athenians believed that Alexander, unlike his father Philip II of Macedon, was too young and weak and would not dare to cross the borders of Macedonia. Hence, they were impatient to breach the reluctant alliance they had previously made with Philip. During August 336 B.C., about a year after Alexander's accession to the throne, the Athenian Demosthenes, paid by the Persian king Darius III, initiated a rebellion against Alexander. Darius III, who had celebrated the murder of Philip II as a positive event for Persia, started to get uncomfortable with Alexander's success. Demosthenes was probably not the only Greek who received payments from the Persian king to rebel against Alexander.

Demosthenes not only advocated a war against Macedonia, but he also presented a false witness who allegedly had fought side by side with Alexander and who asserted that the Macedonian king died in a battle near the Danube, together with half of his army. Demosthenes convinced numerous Thebans living in Athens, exiled by Alexander a year before, to return to Thebes and start a rebellion. Without fighting, Thebes had surrendered to Alexander about a year before, and he had sent to Athens those who initiated the rebellion. Demosthenes provided the rebels with money and promised them the support of Athens, in case of misfortune.

The deported Thebans agreed; they arrived secretly at night in Thebes, killed the Macedonians' guards, and the following morning they proclaimed their uprising against Macedonia. This insurrection encouraged other Greek cities, like Athens, which took advantage of the situation and changed its neutral position. Athens called for a Hellenic crusade against Macedonia. The Athenians went even further and started to negotiate an alliance with the Persian king. At that point, a Greco-Persian alliance against Macedonia was imminent.

Alexander, who had just defeated the Illyrian king at the Illyrian marshes, received the report of the riot by September of that same year, 335 B.C. He decided to eliminate the Greek revolution with remarkable speed. He did not go back to Macedonia from the Illyrian marshes, but instead he headed directly to Thebes. In a tremendous effort, Alexander covered 200 miles mostly through mountains and hills. On the fourteenth day of advance, Alexander and his army, consisting of more than 30,000 warriors, were at the gates of Thebes.

The Thebans were astonished. Not only was Alexander alive, he was standing right at their city walls. They tried to convince themselves this was not Alexander the Great, but his General Antipater leading the Macedonian troops. Alexander expected the Thebans to send him ambassadors to negotiate a peace treaty and to surrender. That, however, did not happen. Though some Thebans wanted to surrender, others were reluctant. Unfortunately, for the future of Thebes, the insubordinate ones had more influence than those who wanted to negotiate and surrender.

The Thebans were successfully defending their city, but then General Antipater brought the reserve army into the battle. Alexander discovered a postern in the city walls and sent his friend Perdicas to seize it. These two new offensives were crucial; the Thebans could not resist the combined attack, and the Macedonians entered the city.

Alexander's allies voted to punish severely the city because of its betrayal of Macedonia and friendship with the Persians. Alexander agreed and razed the city to the ground, as a lesson to all the other Greek cities that contemplated insurrection. Except for the priests, some friends of the Macedonians, and those who had opposed the war, Alexander either killed the Thebans or sold them into slavery. Therefore, Thebes disappeared from the face of the earth in the second half of 335 B.C. Alexander's prodigious speed proved decisive.

During that first year of his reign, Alexander punished the assassin of his father. Additionally he eliminated the pretenders to the crown of Macedonia, gained the submission and respect of the Macedonian army, extended the Macedonian kingdom to the Danube, defeated the Illyrian king, eliminated the Theban insurrection, and regained the Hellenic leadership!

Setting a Fast Pace

After the Granicus Battle, 334 B.C., Alexander marched toward Ephesus, where he offered a sacrifice to Artemis, the Greek moon goddess. Then he advanced in the direction of Miletus and took the outer city without a blow being struck.

Officer Hegisistratus, appointed by Dario to defend the city, had written to Alexander earlier offering his capitulation, but now the nearness of the Persian navy encouraged Hegisistratus to try to save the city. Trying to buy some time, he asked for neutrality for Miletus in the war, but Alexander rejected this new proposal.

Instead, Alexander reacted to this unexpected situation at once by sending the Greek navy—commanded by Nicanor—to Miletus. The maneuver was too fast for Hegisistratus and the Persian navy. Nicanor arrived in Miletus just three days before the Persian fleet, and he anchored his 160 ships at Lade—an island just off the town. Alexander then sent a contingent of Thracians and mercenaries onto dry land to reinforce Lade's defenses.

The Persians' commanders, surprised by this fast maneuver, decided to anchor their 400 ships under Mount Mycale, close to the Greek fleet. Parmenio wanted to engage in a naval battle, but Alexander overruled his advice again because he wished to win the sea battle from land. Alexander then sent his siege engines (large machines designed to break city walls and other fortifications) and started to shoot at the walls of Miletus. After the assault had begun, Nicanor directed his ships toward the harbor of Miletus and repositioned them in the narrowest part of the entrance, very close to one another, closing the port to the Persian fleet and keeping the city isolated.

Before long, Alexander took the town and changed his attention to the men who had escaped to a little island. He also sent mounted troops to prevent the Persian fleet from getting onto land, depriving the Persian navy of water and other supplies. The Persians then sailed for the island of Samos, acquired new supplies, and returned to Miletus.

In a last attempt to win, the Persian fleet adopted battle positions to provoke the Macedonians, while five of their ships moved secretly into *protected* water, between the island of Lade and the

Macedonian army on the shore. The idea was to surprise Alexander's ships with few marines aboard and burn the vessels. Part of the Greek crew was actually gone on assignment to various tasks, but when Alexander saw the five Persian ships approaching, he sent ten of his own vessels with instructions to smash into the enemy ones. The captains of the five Persian ships noticed this quick maneuver and raced back to rejoin their fleet, but one of the ships did not make it. Alexander's speed helped him win the sea battle from the land, as he predicted.

After forcing the Cilician Gates in the summer of 333 B.C., Alexander learned that Arsames, governor of Cilicia, had abandoned his initial plan of defending the city of Tarsus. Apparently, Arsames' new intention after discerning that Alexander had passed the gates was to abandon the town and to strip it before leaving, so Alexander would not find any provisions for his army.

Alexander took immediate action to stop Arsames. He brought a lightly armed detachment, marched at maximum speed even in great heat, and moved down about 3,000 feet into an unventilated plain. Upon their arrival at Tarsus, the Macedonians were exhausted. Arsames, aware of their fast approach, had not risked halting to strip Tarsus. Arsame instead hurried to the court of Darius.

Speed in Critical Situations

After defeating Darius at Issus in November 333 B.C., Alexander proceeded to the siege of Tyre and Gaza and took over both cities in only ten months, an achievement of caliber and speed that no other general of ancient history would repeat.

At the beginning of the year 330 B.C., soon after he had defeated Ariobarzanes, satrap of the Persian province, Alexander traveled to Persepolis. Aware of the vast wealth held at Persepolis, he advanced at maximum speed toward the city.

The defense forces did not have time to steal the city's fortune before the Macedonian king arrived. Thanks to his quickness, Alexander captured not only the riches of Persepolis (about 120,000 talents[†]), but also the wealth of Cyrus the First (about 6,000 talents) kept at the city of Pasargadae—the old capital of Persia.

By May of 330 B.C., after finding that Darius was in Media, Alexander left Persepolis and headed north, taking control of Paraetacae on his way to fight Darius. The Macedonian king then received a new report indicating that Darius had received backup troops from Scythia and Cadusia and had decided to fight him again. In view of that information, Alexander marched at full speed in battle arrangement, leaving the baggage wagons and stores with their guards, who followed at a slower pace.

Alexander reached Media in twelve days, and there he learned that Darius had not actually received his reinforcements yet. For that reason, Darius decided to back away. Alexander then increased the pace of his chase, putting his troops under severe strain. Approximately three days later, Bisthanes, the son of Darius' predecessor, met Alexander and informed him about Darius'

---

† One talent was about fifty-seven and a half pounds weight of gold or silver.

recent retreat five days before. Bisthanes further informed Alexander that the Persian king was taking with him the treasures from Media, and approximately 3,000 equestrians and 6,000 infantry.

When Alexander reached Ecbatana (currently Hamadan, Iran), he dismissed a large number of his troops and sent them back to the Aegean. General Parmenio was instructed to stay in Ecbatana, and that was the last time Alexander would see his general. Without any delay, Alexander marched north in pursuit of Darius for eleven days. So furious was his speed that many of his men dropped out exhausted, and a number of horses galloped to death. Nevertheless, Alexander did not slow down the pace. In eleven days, he reached Rhagae, just about one day away from the Caspian Gates, which Darius had already crossed.

Disappointed, Alexander stopped and rested in Rhagae (south of what is now Tehran, Iran) for five days. Several of Darius' soldiers had deserted, and many others surrendered to Alexander. At this point, Alexander received two Babylonians who informed him that Nabarzanes, Darius' own commander, had betrayed and arrested Darius with help from the satraps Bessus and Barsaentes. Alexander rushed east immediately to capture the traitors, taking with him merely the Companions, the advance scouts, and some of the best members of the light infantry. These troops carried their weapons and provisions for only two days. The remaining troops, led by Craterus, followed Alexander at their own speed. During two days, Alexander marched day and night, stopping only at noon to rest during the high temperature.

When Alexander reached Darius' last camp, he confirmed the version he had received about the Persian king's arrest. He also learned that Bessus, satrap of Bactria, who assumed power in his place, had taken Darius captive in a wagon. His horses and men already worn out, Alexander continued the chase. After a swift march that lasted the entire night and morning, he arrived at noon at a village where Bessus and Darius had stopped only one day before.

There he learned that his enemies had decided to proceed at night too, so he asked the natives for a shortcut to save some time. The shortcut was deserted and without access to water, but Alexander decided to take it anyway, replacing nearly 500 equestrians with light infantry. The king then led the chase one more time between sunset and sunrise through a fifty-mile saline road, until they approached the Persians at last.

With Alexander that close, Nabarzanes and Barsaentes decided to stab Darius, leaving him in the wagon and escaping with Bessus and 600 horsemen. Only sixty soldiers remained with Alexander when he finally found Darius. The Persian king had died shortly before his lifetime enemy could see him, and his traitors had escaped. In slightly more than a week, Alexander had traveled around 230 miles in the summer heat and through a desert.

Alexander arrived in Susia, a town near the border of the province of Aria, in 330/329 B.C. While there he received the visit of Satibarzanes, satrap of Aria. And after confirming the latter in his office, Alexander sent him back in the custody of the Companion Anaxippus and forty men. Soon after this episode,

Alexander received a report from certain Persians that the satrap Bessus had declared himself king of Asia and successor of Darius. Bessus already had the support of the Persian troops who had escaped with him to Bactria after killing Darius, plus a significant number of Bactrians, and he was waiting to receive additional armed forces from Scythia.

Knowing Bessus' plans, Alexander headed to Bactria with his entire army. However, on his way there, he was informed that Satibarzanes had killed Anaxippus and was arming the Arians with clear intentions of joining Bessus. Aware of the threat that this union of forces would represent to his aspirations, the Macedonian changed his route and advanced at high speed to fight Satibarzanes and the Arians, taking with him the Companions, the Agrianes, mounted troops, archers, and two battalions. Alexander left Craterus in command of the rest of the troops.

Fig. 4. Bust of Alexander the Great.[6]

In only two days, Alexander and his army reached Artacoana after walking more than seventy-five miles. Such speed took Satibarzanes so much by surprise that the Arian could only run away. A few mounted troops escaped with Satibarzanes. Most of his men, however, deserted and attempted to escape, but they were quickly tracked down and killed or sold into slavery. Again, Alexander's proverbial speed to respond to challenges had played a decisive role in his success.

Chapter III

Beyond Passion

"His [Alexander's] passion was for glory only, and in that he was insatiable."[1] *Arrian*

SOMETHING EVEN MORE intense than passion moved Alexander; obsession drove him. From a young age, he believed that he was destined to become the master of the world. This pathological obsession not only persisted but also increased throughout his life. His lack of interest in ordinary pleasures was evident from his childhood. They barely tempted him, and he used them with impressive moderation. In contrast, he was passionate in his pursuit of glory.

Alexander's obsession with long-lasting glory helped him endure transitory hardships for the sake of achieving longer-than-life goals. He was always proud of the war wounds he received and the hardships he had to face, because he saw them as part of the price of glory—as hallmarks of sacrifice, merit, and courage. His supreme self-confidence inspired his army as much as it worried his enemies, but on occasions, it influenced him against his better judgment and put him and his people in very risky situations.

Enduring Hardships

Alexander was sixteen years old when he and his father Philip II, king of Macedonia, were returning to Pella (then capital of Macedonia) after Alexander's first exploit, near the Danube River. While passing through the territory of the Medes, the tribes from that hostile land attacked the Macedonians, and a lance thrown against Philip killed his horse and struck him in the leg. Alexander immediately jumped from his horse and covered his father's body with his shield until other soldiers came to the assistance of the king. While Philip's injury was not serious, it left him with a permanent difficulty to walk.

Later in his life, Philip lamented about this injury and other wounds that he had received during his campaigns—such as a blind eye and a fracture in his back. The young prince could not understand his father's laments. He would ask Philip how he could possibly complain about those wounds since they constantly reminded the king and everyone else of his bravery and glory.

As the historian Arrian wrote, "Alexander's passion was for glory only, and in that he was insatiable." Alexander renounced immediate gratifications for the benefit of obtaining everlasting glory. Just before starting his unthinkable campaign aimed at conquering the world, Alexander donated all his possessions—from lands and domains to privileges and income rights—to his friends.

Alexander was a firm believer in preserving his discipline and moderation even after accomplishing major successes. He did not like the new way of living that some of his close friends had adopted after they defeated the Persians. Hagnon, for instance, started to wear silver nails in his shoes, Leonnatus used several camels just to bring him powder from Egypt, and many others started to use precious ointments to bathe; or they brought servants all over the world to rub them and to wait on them in their chambers. When Alexander noticed that his own people had become lavish and excessive, he criticized them gently but firmly.

He told them he wondered how they, who had been engaged in so many single battles, did not know by experience that those who labor, sleep more sweetly and soundly than those who are labored for. How could they fail to see by comparing the Persians' manner of living with their own that it was the most abject and slavish condition to be voluptuous, but the most noble and royal to undergo pain and labor. "Are you still to learn," asked Alexander, "that the end and perfection of our victories is to avoid the vices and infirmities of those whom we subdue?"[2]

Then, to emphasize his principles by walking his talk, Alexander engaged more than ever in hunting and physical activities, taking on any occasion that would cause him privation and danger. As Napoleon Bonaparte would later say, "The first virtue in a soldier is endurance of fatigue; courage is only the second virtue."

To convince his soldiers to advance further and make additional sacrifices, Alexander addressed them in the following manner:

> *If you have any complaint to make about the results of your efforts hitherto, or about myself as your commander, there is no more to say. But let me remind you: through your courage and endurance you have gained possession of Ionia, the Hellespont, both Phrygias, Cappadocia, Paphlagonia, Lydia, Caria, Lycia Pamphylia, Phoenicia, and Egypt; the Greek part of Libya is now yours, together with much of Arabia, lowland Syria, Mesopotamia, Babylon, and Susia; Persia and Media with all the territories either formerly controlled by them or not are in your hands; you have made yourselves masters of the land beyond the Caspian Gates, beyond the Caucasus, beyond the Tanais, of Bactria, Hyrcania, and the Hyrcanian Sea; we have driven the Scythians back into the desert; and Indus and Hydaspes, Acesines and Hydraotes flow now through country which is ours.[3]*

Later he added:

> *Come, then; add the rest of Asia to what you already possess—a small addition to the great sum of your conquests. What great or noble work could we ourselves have achieved had we thought it enough, living at ease in Macedon, merely to guard our homes,*

accepting no burden beyond checking the encroachment or the
Thracians on our borders, or the Illyrians and Triballians, or
perhaps such Greeks as might prove a menace to our comfort?
I could not have blamed you for being the first to lose heart if
I, your commander, had not shared in your exhausting marches
and your perilous campaigns; it would have been natural enough
if you had done all the work merely for others to reap the reward.
But it is not so. You and I, gentlemen, have shared the labor and
shared the danger, and the rewards are for us all.[4]

Alexander was a frenetic fighter, so obsessed with glory that a few times he lost his control during the rage of battles, paying no attention to his own safety. The utter pleasure of combat was sometimes uncontrollable for him.

Influence of Mentors and Role Models

One of the richest persons in the world and arguably the world's greatest investor, Warren Buffet, said that the best thing he did was to choose the right heroes.[5] Role models and mentors who inspired and motivated Alexander influenced his life. From a tender age, he showed great love for the Iliad. He would read Homer's verses over and over to learn more about his favorite hero, Achilles.

In the year 343 B.C., his father Philip invited the philosopher Aristotle, probably the most educated and celebrated philosopher of those times, to Macedonia and asked him to school his son. Aristotle accepted the offer and moved to Stagira, Philip's hometown, where the king had built facilities for Alexander's and other nobles' education. The philosopher motivated them to achieve excellence through constant practice. "We are what we repeatedly do," said Aristotle. "Excellence then, is not a single act, but a habit."[6] Noting Alexander's devotion to Homer, Aristotle prepared a revised version of the Iliad as a gift to the young Macedonian prince. Alexander esteemed Aristotle's gift as an ideal guide to military matters, and he carried it around the world, rereading it regularly and tucking it under his pillow every night together with his knife.

Just before starting his stupendous campaign in Asia, Alexander crossed the Hellespont and arrived in Troy by the year 334 B.C. He was especially interested in visiting the grave of Achilles and honoring him. Tradition has it that Hephaestion, Alexander's dearest friend and perhaps lover, laid a wreath on the tomb of Patroclus, Achilles' closest friend, while Alexander placed one on the tomb of Achilles.*

Alexander also honored the memory of other heroes buried at that place and offered sacrifices for Priam, the old Trojan king and father of the brave Hector. Before fighting the Persians, Alexander walked through the places where the walls of Troy once stood, where the legendary battles took place, and where Achilles fought Hector. Alexander considered Achilles very lucky to have had loyal friends while he lived and an eminent poet like Homer to proclaim his accomplishments after his death.

---

*In the Hellenic culture, it was common and socially accepted for a man to have a male lover, so long as he was the active person.

Aristotle was Alexander's instructor and mentor on the subjects of political science, oratory, grammar, natural science, philosophy, astronomy, medicine, and geometry. The philosopher also taught analysis to Alexander. The student had a high regard for his professor and was aware that he and his friends had acquired knowledge from Aristotle that was not available to other people.

Some years later, when Alexander was fighting in a remote part of the world, he learned that Aristotle had published books revealing the precious knowledge that he and his close friends had received directly from the philosopher. Alexander did not like the idea that his mentor had made the unique education available to other people.

Fig. 5. Aristotle.[7]

Another role model of Alexander was Cyrus the Younger, who had started an expedition with Xenophon in the year 401 B.C. with the intention of seizing the Persian Empire, then ruled by his brother Artaxerxes II. Xenophon, in his book *Anabasis* (Greek for expedition), tells us that Cyrus hired about 13,000 Greek mercenaries, known as the Ten Thousands, to undertake the expedition against his brother. Alexander studied the *Anabasis*, of course, and used Cyrus' experience in Asia as a reference for his initial steps into this land, which was new for him and his people.

Always an Opponent

Alexander always had a rival to defeat, a land to conquer, or a battle—political or military—to win. His first rival, more imaginary than real, was his own father, Philip II of Macedonia. After Philip's death, Alexander shifted his focus to other opponents, like Prince Amyntas, Demosthenes, Memnon of Rhodes, Darius III, Satibarzanes, Bessus, and King Porus. Each rival was a new milestone in Alexander's path to everlasting glory.

Alexander saw a rival in Philip because he believed that his father's conquests would lessen his own future accomplishments. His obsession for honor and endless glory was such that he preferred to receive a kingdom in trouble, where he would have to prove his courage and superiority, rather than one already prosperous and settled, where he would have a sedentary life surrounded by riches and comfort.

One day, a Thessalian named Philonicus brought a horse to Philip and tried to sell it to the king for thirteen talents, but every time Philip's attendants tried to mount it, the horse reared. After a while, the attendants gave up and determined that the horse was useless. Then Alexander, who had observed all of the foregoing, said, "What an excellent horse do they lose for want of address and boldness to manage him!"

Only after the young prince had repeated the same statement several times, did Philip respond to him. And the following conversation took place:

Philip: *"Do you reproach those who are older than yourself, as if you knew more, and were better able to manage him than they?"*
Alexander: *"I could manage this horse better than others do."*
Philip: *"And if you do not, what will you forfeit for your rashness?"*
Alexander: *"The whole price of the horse.*[8]*"*

The entire company laughed at Alexander's last comment, but not for long, because the prince ran at once toward the horse, grabbed its bridle and turned it toward the sun, for he had observed that the animal was disturbed by the movement of its own large shadow. Then he let the horse move forward a little and mounted it with one quick jump, drew the bridle little by little, and curbed the horse without striking it or spurring it. As soon as Alexander noticed less resistance from the horse, he let it go at full speed and encouraged it to run even faster.

When Alexander returned with the horse, Philip and his friends were staring astonished at the prince. The king then said to Alexander, "O my son, look for a kingdom equal to and worthy of thyself, for Macedonia is too little for thee."[9] From that day on, Philip started to persuade Alexander, rather than directing him to do anything. The name of that powerful animal was Bucephalus, the legendary horse that would serve Alexander during most of his battles.

Fig. 6. Alexander Training Bucephalus.[10]

Later in life, Alexander and Philip participated in a more serious fight that almost ended the life of one of them. Numerous differences between Olympia, Alexander's mother, and Philip ruined their marriage. And soon Philip fell in love with Cleopatra, a beautiful woman younger than Olympia. During the wedding of Philip and Cleopatra, her drunken uncle, Attalus, wished that Macedonians would ask the gods to give them a lawful successor to the kingdom through Cleopatra. This he said because Olympia was originally from Epirus, a barbarian[†] for Macedonians, while Cleopatra was a noble Macedonian. Furthermore, Olympia had said that on the night of Alexander's conception she had a dream in which she had sexual relations with the god Zeus, and for that reason, she often claimed that Alexander was not the son of Philip.

Attalus' words irritated Alexander so much that he threw his cup of wine at the head of Attalus while exclaiming, "You villain, what am I, then, a bastard?"[11] Philip rose up, took his sword and advanced in the direction of Alexander with the intention to kill him. No one dared to stop him but, luckily for Philip and Alexander, the drunken king slipped and fell on the floor, upon which Alexander said, "See there, the man who makes preparations to pass out of Europe into Asia, overturned in passing from one seat to another."[12] After this episode, Alexander took his mother to Epirus, and then he retired into Illyria (region of southern Europe in the Balkan Peninsula).

After a short time, the Corinthian Demaratus, an old friend of the family, visited Philip. When asked by the king whether the Grecians were at peace with each other, he replied, "It ill becomes you, to be solicitous about Greece, when you have involved your own house in so many dissensions and calamities."[13] Philip recognized his mistake and asked his son to come back home, and by Demaratus' intervention, Alexander and his mother returned to Pella.

[†] It is interesting to note that Macedonians considered barbarians the people from some countries, especially northern kingdoms, but they did not like to be regarded as such by the Greeks, a more civilized southern population.

The king of kings, Darius III, was Alexander's most serious rival. Alexander's obsession to fight Darius and capture his huge empire ended only with Darius' death.

During the decisive Battle of Gaugamela against Darius at the end of 331 B.C., the Bactrian cavalry severely attacked the left wing of Alexander's army—led by General Parmenio—and forced it to move back in disorder. All at once, Mazaeus, who was leading the Mesopotamian Syrians, sent a unit around to attack the people who guarded the Macedonian baggage in the back. Parmenio was very concerned and sent messengers to inform Alexander that the encampment and belongings would be lost unless he reinforced the back with a force taken from the front line. Alexander sent a response to Parmenio saying that he must have lost his mind. For if they were successful, they would own all of their enemies' possessions. If defeated, instead of worrying about their belongings, they should fight bravely and die with honor.

Alexander did not consider running away from his enemies as an option. He preferred to die fighting rather than to retreat in disgrace.

He was born to fight and needed to defeat rivals and conquer new territories to feel alive. One could say that he was probably fortunate to die after he had conquered virtually all the known world, for his life would not have had the same meaning afterward.

Alexander's virtue of resilience represented a significant source of referent power for him. Referent power is one of the five sources of power proposed by French and Rave.[14] Referent power is based on an individual's attractiveness to others. People comply with the leader because they respect and like him or her. This source of power does not depend exclusively on the organization or group but rather on the effectiveness of the individual as a role model.

Expert power does not depend exclusively on the organization either. Referent power and expert power tend to cause the highest level of commitment, and several studies have shown that they produce high levels of satisfaction and performance[15] among followers.[16] Alexander's referent power and his other qualities, granted him broad support and understanding from his people who otherwise might not have excused some of his mistakes. They so much valued his virtues that they excused his excesses.

Alexander was insatiable for everlasting glory; and in pursuit of such glory, he risked himself too much and was several times close to death.

Chapter IV

Bold and Clear Goals

"Of all the things I've done, the most vital is coordinating the talents of those who work for us and pointing them toward a certain goal"[1]

Walt Disney

ANY MAJOR CHANGE or achievement starts with a bold goal. "The leader," said the French general and politician Charles De Gaulle, "must aim high, see big, judge widely, thus setting himself apart from the ordinary people who debate in narrow confines."[2] More often than not, however, big goals tend to be vague, lacking in detail and clarity. While some people walk through a reasonable part of their lives lacking clear goals, clarity of purpose in life is an important step on the road to success, for it allows a person to concentrate his or her efforts instead of attempting to do everything.

Michael Porter, professor at Harvard Business School, explains it in plain words: "Strategy is making trade-offs in competing. The essence of strategy is deciding what *not* to do."[3] He goes on: "With so many forces at work against making choices and trade-offs in organizations, a clear intellectual framework to guide strategy is a necessary counterweight. Moreover, strong leaders willing to make choices are essential."[4]

Alexander's obsession pushed him to set extremely ambitious goals for himself and for his people. He believed from a young age that he was destined to become the master of the world, and that obsession not only persisted, but also increased throughout his life. Initially, Alexander's goal seemed to be a borrowed one: to continue his father's ideal of creating a pan-Hellenic union and freeing the Greek cities of Asia Minor from the oppression of the Persian king Darius III. At least, that was what Alexander stated publicly in front of his compatriots and the Greeks. Deep in his mind, he may have already been thinking of something bigger. The truth was that those Greek cities of Asia Minor were not concerned about the Persians' domination. In fact, they had a good life, living in peace and far away from the Persian king. Their perception, however, changed once Alexander started to liberate them from Persian domination.

After subduing Greece and conquering Asia Minor, winning battle after battle, Alexander appeared to change his goals. The more he conquered, the farther he wanted to go. It looked as if nothing could stop the young victorious conqueror—not weather, nor enemies, nor distances to cover.

Alexander's goal was not to capture the treasures of the countries that he conquered. He did not want to get revenge or impose a religion. On the contrary, his initial goal was to free the countries from Persian domination and create a new world where each country would keep its own treasures, religions, and traditions. Then, with unification of the new world, wars would end. The ruler of this new world would, of course, be Alexander.

Having clear goals and a vision of the future is crucial for any leader, but if a leader is not skillful enough at communicating and convincing those who can help him or her achieve those goals, then the vision will never materialize. Alexander had a cloudless vision of what he wanted for himself and his country, and he was masterful in communicating and sharing it with his people. His conviction about the future had a powerful influence on his people, and this conviction made it easier for them to buy into his goals. In a way, the excessive nature of these goals worked like a self-fulfilling prophesy for him, his soldiers, and ultimately his enemies.

Bold and clear goals are the foremost means to stimulate people and to produce results. As Collins and Porras explain in their book, *Built to Last*,[5] "Like a moon mission, a true *big hairy audacious goal* is clear and compelling and serves as a unifying focal point of effort—often creating immense team spirit." They go on: "It engages people—it reaches out and grabs them in the gut. It is tangible, energizing, highly focused. People 'get it' right away; it takes little or no explanation."

Not Compromising Goals

Rudy Giuliani says there are many qualities that make a great leader. However, he adds that having strong beliefs, being able to stick with them through popular and unpopular times, is the most important characteristic of a great leader.[6]

Alexander did not compromise his goals. They were so clear, and he was so certain to attain them, that he would not take any shortcut to realize them if it meant a change in the spirit of the goals. If he considered something was essential, he would fight for as long as it took to attain it.

A good example of his not compromising occurred in July 334 B.C. when Alexander received a proposal from the people of Miletus. The proposal said the Milesians wanted to remain neutral and were willing to allow free use of their harbors and equal access to the city by Alexander and the Persians. Under these terms, they said, the siege of Miletus should stop. Alexander's reply to this proposal was firm:

> *I did not come to Asia to accept what the people want to offer me. I am the only one to decide whether to forgive or punish a city like Miletus, which has failed to honor its promise. I suggest you go back behind your walls and prepare to fight, because I did not come here to hear your proposals, but to tell the Milesians that their city will be taken over soon.*[7]

Alexander sent his siege engines and attacked the walls of Miletus the following dawn. He seized Miletus and ruled it on his own terms.

Alexander's bold and clear goals had very prolonged effects, even though his empire was virtually divided after his death. Without any doubt, Alexander's conquest of the known world contributed to shape the culture and the world as we know it today. It all started with an *insane* goal, which he shared with his people in these words:

> *Our ships will sail round from the Persian Gulf to Libya as far as the Pillars of Heracles,*[*] *whence all Libya to the eastward will soon be ours, and all Asia too, and to this empire there will be no boundaries but what God Himself has made for the whole world.*[8]

"For an idea that does not at first seem insane," said Albert Einstein, "there is no hope."[9]

---

[*]Also called Hercules (the Roman name for the mythical Greek hero Heracles).

Chapter V

Effective Planning

> *"If I always appear prepared, it is because before entering an under-taking, I have meditated long and have foreseen what may occur. It is not genius which reveals to me suddenly and secretly what I should do in circumstances unexpected by others; it is thought and preparation."*[1]   *Napoleon Bonaparte*

THE FOLLOWING DIAGRAM illustrates the relationship of effective planning, attention to details, and resources committed. The worst planning comes out of low attention to details and low utilization of resources—particularly the time devoted, the people involved in the formulation and revision of the plan, and in some cases, the equipment and other resources. This kind of planning, all other things being equal, results in unwanted surprises and high dependence on good fortune. Conversely, the best planning emerges from high attention to detail and high utilization of resources (time, people, and others).

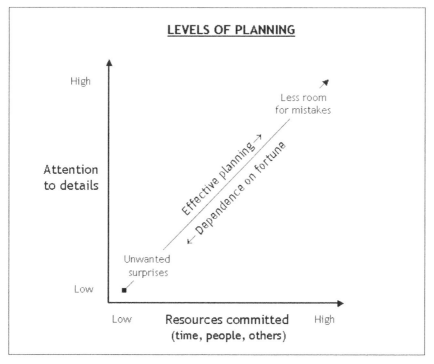

Fig. 7. Levels of Planning.

Alexander became a maestro at the art of planning, gaining comparative advantage to compensate for some of his army's disadvantages. His relentless planning did not end in analysis paralysis but in bold actions.

Details Make a Difference

"Sometimes when I consider what tremendous consequences come from little things," said Bruce Barton, author of many bestselling guides to personal success, "I am tempted to think there are no little things."[2] Alexander knew that the sum of small details makes a big difference. He was a perfectionist who planned every possible detail in order to minimize unexpected events. Typically, he gathered as much information as possible about his enemy, the territory, water and food supplies, weather conditions, and other relevant matters. He learned from his own scouts, natives, and the enemies of his enemies. He used every piece of the puzzle to form the best possible picture of the situation at hand. Then he carefully explored each alternative with the help of his close subordinates, analyzing every fact and listening to all their opinions. After making a decision, he would take care of the final details to reduce the possibilities of unwanted surprises during a battle or a difficult advance.

Knowing the Opponent

From a young age, Alexander developed a keen interest in other kingdoms—especially the powerful ones. He wanted to learn as much as possible about their culture, history, politics, religion, weapons, and war techniques. Around the year 340 B.C., Alexander received a delegation sent by the great king of Persia, Artaxerxes III (Ochus), to Pella, capital of Macedonia. His father Philip had previously signed an important agreement with the

Persians. He had agreed not to support the enemies of the great king in Asia Minor, while the great king agreed not to intervene in Greece—where the Macedonians were threatening Athens and other Greek cities.

The sixteen-year-old Macedonian prince's questions impressed the ambassadors the great king had sent. Alexander asked them numerous questions about the length and nature of their roads, their main cities, the personality of their king, how he behaved with his enemies, and what military force he was capable of putting onto a battlefield.

Alexander liked to hear stories about other civilizations, perhaps envisioning that they would became his rivals at some point in the future. He was very interested in knowing the history of his eventual adversaries. Knowing who the neighbors of his main enemies were and how they related to one another in the past and currently, helped him to identify potential allies and to gain local support: soldiers, food, and logistics.

Alexander explored and exploited the internal political struggles and divisions that his enemies were facing. He would carefully explore each political alternative or combat option before making a decision. Once he had made a decision, however, he did not have second thoughts. Alexander planned every detail, and then he acted fast—very fast.

Preparing for the Unknown

"Prepare for the unknown," said George Patton, "by studying how others in the past have coped with the unforeseeable and the unpredictable."[3] By the end of November 336 B.C., three months after his father's murder and his accession to the throne, Alexander the Great was preparing for his expedition against the Persians. Before embarking on a campaign that he anticipated being long and extremely dangerous, he wanted to secure Macedonia against potential invasions. The northern tribes of Illyrians, Triballians, and Thracians represented the most dangerous threats. The new Macedonian king wanted a clear and solid victory against them before departing for Asia Minor.

During the spring of 335 B.C., Alexander attacked the tribes living in northern Thrace, but the independent Thracians were located at the top of a treacherous mountain, making it very difficult to reach them. Even if the Macedonian troops could pass through the narrow gorges that led to the base of the mountain, it would have been very difficult to climb the mountain and defeat their enemy at the same time. In addition, the Thracians had planned to push their heavy war chariots down the hill once the Macedonian phalanx (a body of heavily armed infantry in close array) had reached a point of no return. Alexander, who had contemplated that possibility among some others, developed a plan to prevent a catastrophe.

He told his soldiers that if the Thracians decided to push their war chariots down the hill, those soldiers who were in a relatively broad path would break their combat formation and avert the chariots. Conversely, those soldiers who were in a narrow place would move forward, elbow to elbow, without leaving any gap between their shields. Due to their speed, the chariots would jump over the soldiers' locked shields without hurting them.

When the Thracians sent down their chariots, Alexander's soldiers were prepared for the maneuver. They moved as Alexander had instructed them, and once they had averted the chariots, the Macedonian infantry attacked the Thracians with violence while the archers kept the Thracians away. After a short battle, the Thracians could no longer resist the combined assault of the infantry and the rain of arrows of the archers, and they ran away, leaving 1,500 casualties in the battlefield.

Timing the Attack

An important part of a good plan is deciding when to attack, for a badly timed action could jeopardize a plan that otherwise would be successful. A good example of a plan well timed was Alexander's attack at Granicus.

Alexander left Pella around April of the year 334 B.C., moving toward Asia with the hilarious idea of conquering the Persian Empire. He did not know about the Persian geography and population, but he did know that the country was huge. He left Antipater in charge of the affairs in Macedonia and Greece with approximately 12,000 infantry and 1,500 cavalry, and headed to Asia with 30,000 infantry and 5,000 cavalry.

After crossing the Hellespont, now known as the Dardanelles, and using 160 triremes and many merchant vessels, Alexander's army advanced toward the river Granicus, led by Parmenio. Alexander took a different route. After passing through Troy, he marched to Arisbe to meet with the main Macedonian army. Then he and the entire army advanced upon the river Granicus in battle order, expecting a combat, with both wings protected by cavalry.

Meanwhile, the Persian commander Memnon of Rhodes had advised his colleagues against fighting Alexander, arguing that the Macedonian infantry was superior in numbers and better trained, and that while Alexander was present in person the Persian King Darius III was not. Memnon recommended devastating the fields before Alexander to endanger his army by lack of supplies for his soldiers and horses, but the Persian command overruled Memnon and decided to attack the invaders.

When the Macedonians finally arrived at the Granicus River, their Persian opponents, commanded by Arsames, were already waiting for them on the opposite side of the river. Alexander gave orders to prepare for the battle, but Parmenio was opposed to the idea and advised his king to halt there because the Persians, outnumbered as they were would not dare to stay close to the Macedonian army all night. As a result, Parmenio said, the Persians would back away during the night, and Alexander would have no problem crossing at first light, before the Persian army could return to its position to fight Alexander.

He argued that if Alexander decided to cross during the afternoon, his army would have to do it in one long column rather than in a broad line, because the river was very deep in several places. The Persian cavalry would be upon the Macedonian soldiers before they could reach the shore.

Alexander listened carefully to the advice of the elderly and experienced Parmenio. He knew that Parmenio had a valid point, but he believed that delaying the attack could also boost the Persians' confidence. Another disadvantage of fighting on the following morning was that the sun would be right in front of his army, making it more difficult for archers and soldiers to see their targets. If he attacked at sunset, the Persians instead of the Macedonians would have to deal with that same problem.

Alexander weighed the different alternatives and finally decided to attack that same day, and by the end of the afternoon, he had attained his first victory in Asia. He decided, however, not to go after the defeated Persian army, for he thought it would be unwise to enter Asia without first securing his power in the region. If he moved to the East, away from the shore, the powerful Persian navy, anchored not far away, could consolidate its power in the coastal cities of Asia Minor, behind Alexander's back.

Alexander possessed an exquisite sense of timing. Another clear example of this was his strategy before the Battle of Gaugamela. Typically, he took risks in his fights, but on that occasion, he did not rush. He sensed that a night fight would be risky; so he decided to halt and keep the gigantic Persian army waiting under arms for another day and night.

Like Alexander, contemporary leaders should execute their strategies at the appropriate time; in some circumstances, delaying an action is the smartest thing to do. The benefits of well-timed actions include the advantage of surprise and the possibility of wearing out one's opponent physically and intellectually.

Minimizing Unwanted Surprises

Because his army was small, Alexander knew that he had no room for mistakes. Necessity forced him to be always watchful for potential attacks and to remain alert to exploit every opportunity he had. As Colin Powell said, "When everyone's mind is dulled or distracted, the leader must be doubly vigilant."[4]

During the summer of 333 B.C., he moved toward the treacherous region of Cilicia. To enter Cilicia he needed to cross through a narrow pathway, called "The Gates," which looked like a fortification made by natives but was actually a natural formation. Steep mountains rising from the sea confined The Gates, making the path so narrow that it could accommodate only four soldiers alongside each other. The Macedonian forces were in a delicate situation; a potential enemy could throw rocks from above and crush them.

Alexander's cautiousness led him to consider this situation as a battle maneuver rather than a tough march. In an effort to prevent unwanted surprises, he sent light troops before the main army to scout the pathways and detect hidden enemies. Additionally, he sent a detachment of archers to occupy the mountain peaks, with specific orders to keep their bows strung. Finally, the Macedonian army crossed the Cilician Gates free of surprises, and afterward

Alexander sent lightly armed troops to prevent the Persians from stripping and burning the city of Tarsus.

Laborious Preparation

The Battle of Issus was one of Alexander's greatest victories. On the morning of November 1, 333 B.C., the Macedonian army marched in classic battle order to fight the Persians at the Issus plain, near the Gulf of Iskenderun (currently southern Turkey). This time, King Darius III himself was leading the Persian army, and when he learned that Alexander was moving forward, he sent about 30,000 cavalry and 20,000 light infantry across the river Pinarus to buy time so he could put his army in battle order. According to historians Arrian and Plutarch, the Persian force totaled 600,000 soldiers, including heavy infantry, Greek mercenaries, mounted troops, and others. Macedonians and their allies were only about 35,000—about 17 Persian soldiers per Macedonian for hand-to-hand battle.

In preparation for a battle that would make history, Alexander was extremely careful in addressing every single detail. He tried to anticipate all the advantages of the Persians and the few chances of the Macedonians.

Alexander preferred the fight to take place in a narrow place that would give his small army an advantage. He led his troops toward Issus and stopped there to decide whether he should move forward or wait for reinforcements from Macedonia. While planning for the battle, Parmenio suggested that the place was ideal for a fight, as the narrow corridor would give Alexander an advantage. In his view, it was crucial for them to stay away from flat ground because the Persians could surround them and catch them in a pincer maneuver. In an open battlefield, he said, Macedonians could become exhausted, as Persian soldiers would persistently come to the front line if they had freedom of movement. Hence, the size of the enemy's army, rather than the enemy's courage, could defeat the Macedonians.

Alexander considered it a wise defense strategy, and he decided to wait for the Persians at the narrowest part of the corridor. In fact, the actual battlefield turned out to be only about one and a half miles wide. He placed the Macedonian phalanx, clearly his strongest unit, in the front line. He commanded the right wing and Parmenio took the left one with the support of Craterus. Nicanor, Parmenio's son, occupied the right wing with other officers next to him—each one leading his own division—and the foot Companions occupied the center.

Alexander instructed Parmenio to extend his unit as far as possible toward the sea to avoid an encircling maneuver from an army that was overwhelmingly larger, and he placed cavalry on both wings: Macedonians and Thessalians on the right wing and Peloponnesians on the left wing. The king placed archers in front of the army, together with Thracians and Cretans, and he sent the Agrianes to oppose the Persian troops located on top of the hill.

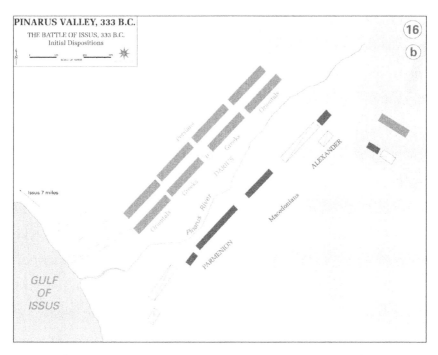

Fig. 8. Courtesy of the Department of History, United States Military Academy.
(Infantry: solid rectangles; cavalry: hollow rectangles)

Alexander ordered his army to advance in classic battle order, in rows of the largest number that the narrow pass would allow. As they advanced, however, the narrows gradually widened, so Alexander commanded his formation to broaden and the cavalry to cover the flanks to avoid encircling maneuvers. Because of this change, the rows of his army went down from sixteen to only eight. The king then went before his army and started gesturing to his people not to hurry. Throughout the battle, he communicated with his soldiers to keep them in order or to change their location.

The battle was long and extremely tough. The night finally found Darius running away from Alexander's army, abandoning his shield, mantle, bow, and chariot. Darius eventually disappeared in the darkness, but 110,000 Persian soldiers lay dead on the battlefield; the Macedonian casualties were about 450 dead and 4,500 wounded. We will go over the details of this battle later.

One of the main differences among professional chess players is the number of moves they are able to contrive from a given position. The more moves a chess player can plan, and the more accurate that planning is, the better the chances he or she has to win. A top-tier player is more likely to foresee an opportunity or a threat before a second-tier player does. By the time the latter sees the danger or the opportunity, it is usually too late to organize a solid defense or to seize the opportunity; hence, the shortsighted player depends more on good fortune to survive than the good planner does. The professional player typically plans for different scenarios because each of his opponent's responses usually results in an entirely new situation.

Although not a professional chess player, Alexander applied very similar concepts in his battlefields and political arenas. As a result, very few situations remained unforeseen to him, and he was able to surprise his opponents on numerous occasions.

Few leaders are willing to make the effort to analyze every possible alternative because they know that most of them will never occur. Nevertheless, the laborious and frequently tedious task of planning as carefully as possible and covering as many alternatives as feasible usually yields big returns. As coach Bear Bryant said, "More than [having] the will to win, you must have the will to prepare to win."[5]

Offensive and Defensive Planning

People frequently underestimate defensive planning because when it is well done, it passes almost unnoticed. Conversely, defensive planning becomes noticeable when failure to prevent a situation has undesired results. A natural tendency is to focus more on offensive planning than on defensive planning. Ironically, that is the opposite of what's advisable because a serious failure in defensive planning can make offensive preparation useless.

Alexander was always meticulous in his defensive planning. Soon after Darius was killed, Alexander divided his forces in three units and advanced toward the province of Hyrcania in pursuit of Bessus—who had acquired power in Darius' place—and his supporters. Alexander went by the shortest and most difficult road, taking with him his largest and lightest unit. He sent Erigyius—with other units and baggage—by the longest and easiest road, and he dispatched Craterus against the Tapurians.

Although Alexander was on the offensive, he did not overlook the defense of his troops. After crossing the first hills, he stopped and decided to continue ahead of the main formation with some archers and a light Macedonian unit. The road was tough and very treacherous, as the hills along the path could have concealed enemies. Alexander, concerned about the safety of the troops behind him, left some of his men to occupy the places that he considered unsafe. No enemy attacked the main formation as they went through the pass, and the soldiers finally reached a safe piece of open land near a little river.

Alexander used defensive planning not only in war maneuvers, but also in politics and internal affairs. After Philotas' debatable complicity in a secret plan to kill Alexander, which ended with the execution of Philotas and his father Parmenio, the king decided to make some changes in the organization of the Companions. He split the Companions' cavalry into two different parts to avoid concentration of power. The Companions were the most powerful unit of the mounted troops, and Alexander thought it was not wise to keep them under the control of a single man—even if that man was a close friend. Therefore, he appointed Hephaestion, his dearest friend, and Cleitus, who had saved Alexander's life during the Granicus Battle, to lead those two powerful units.

Unrelenting planning was one of Alexander's foremost virtues. His life also followed a detailed plan. From his early days, he believed that he was destined to become the ruler of the world and projected his life accordingly. He continued to design and review his master plan periodically until he accomplished it. And afterward, he began to plan how to go beyond the frontiers of the known world. Alexander broke down his master plan into smaller milestones and planned each one of them thoroughly. However, he did not allow the smaller milestones to make him forget about his ultimate goal.

Chapter VI

Leading through Example and Inspiration

"A man should practice what he preaches, but a man should also preach what he practices."[1]   *Confucius*

IN HIS BOOK *Managing with Power,* Jeffrey Pfeffer asks this interesting question: "If the power that derives from positions and formal authority is something granted by others to the occupant of the position, the next question is what motivates social organizations and their members to make such grants?" He goes on, "Why do people obey, rather than challenge, question, or ignore authority...?"[2]

A critical success factor for good leaders is the ability to pull followers instead of pushing them. Although pushing people becomes necessary on occasion, we should consider it an exception rather than a rule; motivating followers by conveying values and being a role model shows better long-term results than other methods.

Alexander led his people to conquer the world by using one of the most effective leadership tools: providing the example. He did not ask from his soldiers anything that he would not do himself. Furthermore, he tried to do more than the rest, sometimes pushing the limits of what others considered humanly possible. Alexander did not need to make the same sacrifices that his soldiers did—needless to say, additional efforts—for he was the king. Alexander was entitled to request sacrifices from them, but he knew that in the long run *the carrot wins over the stick.*

He understood the enormous advantage of leading through example, showing others—soldiers and enemies—his relentless labor and courage. As a result, the Macedonians did not just follow orders from their leader, they admired him because he was a soldier like them. And in many ways, Alexander was better than they were. Not one of them could say that something was too dangerous or too demanding, if their king himself was doing it.

The Macedonian army could not complain about hardships, which their enemies oftentimes considered not humanly possible to endure, because their own king was going through the same deprivations. They could not complain about the risks of battles where the enemy outnumbered them greatly, because the same person who led them to those fields was fighting in the front line facing even more danger than they were. Alexander reminded his soldiers of this in the following words:

There are epicures among you who, I fancy, eat more luxuriously than I; and this I know, that I wake earlier than you—and watch, that you may sleep.

Perhaps you will say that, in my position as your commander, I had none of the labours and distress which you had to endure to win for me what I have won. But does any man among you honestly feel that he has suffered more for me than I have suffered for him? Come now—if you are wounded, strip and show your wounds, and I will show you mine. There is no part of my body but my back which has not a scar; not a weapon a man may grasp or fling the mark of which I do not carry upon me. I have sword-cuts from close fight; arrows have pierced me, missiles from catapults bruised my flesh; again and again I have been struck by stones or clubs—and all for your sakes: for your glory and your gain. Over every land and sea, across river, mountain, and plain I led you to the world's end, a victorious army.[3]

The fact that Alexander had the energy of the best-trained soldiers and exercised with his people regularly had a significant impact on his soldiers. Despite being a successful king, he often dressed like an ordinary citizen, particularly before he defeated the Persians. His behavior inspired his soldiers, and he quickly gained the respect and admiration of the experienced generals and commanders of Macedonia.

Alexander knew how and when to inspire his soldiers. He knew his people thoroughly and, through time, Alexander developed a keen sense of their fears, their problems, and their needs. He would address his people with precise and encouraging words or actions to inspire them for battle. His optimism and calmness were contagious and were deliberately shown in situations where everyone was expecting the worst. Similarly, his rage and courage during combats and pursuits dragged the rest along and spread among his people like a fire. The king's timing to inspire his troops was exquisite, and his words and actions were firm.

Alexander's qualities gave him a great source of *expert* and *referent power*.[4] These two sources of power are related to the individual as a role model[5] and tend to induce the highest level of commitment, performance, and satisfaction among followers.[6]

Conveying Values

"A genuine leader," said Martin Luther King Jr., "is not a searcher for consensus but a molder of consensus."[7] Great leaders, almost invariably, have a unique ability to motivate their followers to achieve higher goals, convincing them to trade current temporary satisfaction for future long-lasting rewards.

In their book *Leaders: Strategies for Taking Charge,* Warren Bennis and Burt Nanus make the following appropriate distinction between a leader and a manager: "The leader operates on the *emotional and spiritual resources* of the organization, on its values, commitment and aspirations. The manager, by contrast, operates on the *physical resources* of the organization, on its capital, human skills, raw materials and technology."[8] While Alexander managed his physical resources masterfully, what really set him apart was his uncanny ability to operate on the emotional and spiritual resources of his army. He did not have many options either. He was king of a relatively poor country, his physical resources were limited, and he knew those resources would not give him an advantage over his powerful enemies.

Alexander did not fight for money; neither did he want to conquer the world for treasures. Money and gold represented sources of power and means to help him achieve his goals, but riches per se, he said, would only make people lazy. From the very beginning, Alexander wanted his soldiers to understand and to accept this concept. He wanted to convey to them that the only thing that mattered was glory. Although money would help them and their families back in Macedonia, they should fight and die for pride and glory, not for gold.

As usual, Alexander did not just preach his belief, but he acted accordingly. He departed from Macedonia to conquer the world with a small army of approximately 30,000 foot soldiers and 4,000 horsemen, having only thirty days' supplies for his troops and seventy talents for their pay. In addition, the king had used almost all the royal property to start the campaign and owed about 800 talents.

Alexander could not afford to offer his people a financial reward, so he motivated them by making them feel like partners in his dream. He donated his patrimony—from lands and domains to privileges and income rights—to his friends. Perdicas, one of the Companions, asked the young king what he would keep for himself after donating all his possessions. "The hope," was Alexander's response. Alexander's close friends were so impressed that they decided to imitate their leader's example by donating their possessions and keeping only the hope for glory. "Your soldiers," said Perdicas, "will be your partners."

Example in the Scene of Action

Alexander's leadership qualities increased during critical times and rough circumstances. During battles, particularly, he showed his soldiers and his enemies uncommon courage and determination, fighting in the front line and risking his life more than his soldiers' lives, as every man in the enemy's line hoped for himself the honor of killing the Macedonian king.

Alexander was short for a warrior, and he did not have an impressive figure. Nevertheless, he was always on the offensive, eager to fight, and constantly looking for a face-to-face confrontation with the leader of his enemies. It was difficult for his soldiers to protect their king because of his fast and risky movements, and because his unique and conspicuous war outfit made it easy for everyone, including enemies, to spot him. His disregard for danger and his courage in difficult situations inspired his people and spread terror among his opponents.

A good example of Alexander's leadership in combat took place in the Granicus Battle. When he arrived at the Granicus River around April-June 334 B.C., intending to cross into Asia Minor, the Persian army led by Arsames was already awaiting him on the opposite side of the river. The Persians presented a very broad position along the other bank, with their cavalry in the front and the infantry in the rear. Memnon and Arsames, governor of Cilicia, the ancient province of Persia in southeast Asia Minor, led the left side. Next to them were Arsites, ruler of Phrygia, leading the Paphlagonia cavalry, and Spithridates, ruler of Ionia, leading the Hyrcanian equestrians. Rheomithres was in charge of the Persian right wing.

A long pause came before the battle. After a deliberation regarding the best timing for the battle, Alexander sent Parmenio to lead the left wing with the Thessalian cavalry while he moved down to the right. Then Amyntas led the advanced scouts into the water and soon faced a battery of missiles from the Persians situated on high ground. Alexander's mounted troops had great difficulty in getting out of the river, and the first to make it to the bank were killed. Then Alexander, leading the right wing, with trumpets blaring, advanced into the river at the head of his men and soon joined battle with Persian commanders, causing serious casualties in the Persian lines.

He spotted Mithridates, Darius' son-in-law, who was leading the Hyrcanian cavalry in an attack against the Macedonians. Alexander then moved ahead of his soldiers toward Mithridates and struck the Persian in the face with a spear, sending him to the ground. The Persian commander Rhoesaces attacked Alexander and sliced part of his helmet off, but Alexander recovered from the impact and struck a spear into Rhoesaces' body armor, piercing his breast. Another Persian commander, Spithridates, charged against Alexander from behind when Cleitus, called "the black," cut Rhoesaces' arm before he could strike.[*]

---

[*]Historians differ on minor details of this episode. The author followed Arrian's version.

The Persians began to break right where Alexander was fighting, and once the center broke, both wings of their cavalry broke as well. By the afternoon, Alexander had secured a clear victory: about 20,000 Persian infantries and 2,500 equestrians were killed, and 2,000 were taken prisoner. Alexander lost twenty-five Companions, sixty equestrians, and thirty infantries.

Alexander won this first battle in Persian territory, essential for the entire campaign, mostly due to his courage and example. Throughout the battle, he had faced various dangers and suffered a minor wound to his scalp. In addition, he received two strikes in his breastplate, three in his shield, and one in his helmet.

Time passed and Alexander won victory after victory in Asia Minor. Neither Darius nor his generals understood how this twenty-two-year-old leader was capable of such achievements. They could not comprehend how the same army that a year before had lost every battle, when Philip was their king, was now winning every single fight with the same soldiers and the same general—Parmenio. What had happened to those Macedonian soldiers? The only thing that had actually changed was their leader. Philip II of Macedonia, a brave warrior, used to guide them, but now they had an unparalleled leader who believed that everything was possible for them. This obsessive young man from a poor nation had somehow convinced his soldiers to follow him to the frontiers of the known world.

Alexander's inspirational skills were evident at Issus, where his morale and his leadership played a vital role to win that epic battle. Right before the fight he gave a precise and impressive speech to his soldiers, reminding them of their past glories and long-standing valor, addressing each one of his commanders by name and title. They were, he said to them, the liberators of the world, and one day they would cross the border set by Heracles and rule the Persians and all the races of the world.

He reminded his people that danger had already threatened them, but they had always ended victorious. This time, he said, the struggle would be against an army they had already defeated. In reality, they had only defeated the Persians at Granicus River, but not Darius and his vast army.

Alexander told his soldiers that God had favored them in making Darius leave the flat grounds and crowd his great army into a reduced space. As a result, Macedonians and their allies would have space to deploy their army and the Persian superiority in numbers would not prevail.

Alexander went on, saying his enemies were no match for his people, neither in strength nor in determination. "They," said Alexander, "are Medes and Persians, men who for centuries have lived soft and luxurious lives; we of Macedon for generations past have been trained in the hazard school of danger and war. Above all, we are free men, and they are slaves. There are Greek troops, to be sure, in Persian service—but how different is their cause from ours! They will be fighting for pay—and not much of it at that; we, on the contrary, shall fight for Greece, and our hearts will be in it. As for our foreign troop—Thracians, Paeonians, Illyrians, Agrianes—they are the best and stoutest soldiers in Europe, and they will find as their opponents the slackest and softest of the tribes of Asia. And what, finally, of the two men in supreme command? You have Alexander, they—Darius!"[9]

After stressing the advantages that they would have in the battle, Alexander told his people that the rewards of their victory would be significant. This time they would be fighting King Darius III of Persia in person, and his army—not his subordinates. Therefore, when the battle ended, they would be ruling over Medes, Persians, and all other Asian people.

Followers tend to like those leaders who make them feel good about themselves. Alexander made his soldiers feel proud of their past and hopeful toward their future. He reminded his people of what they had already achieved together, bringing up every action of bravery, naming persons, and indicating what they had accomplished. He also recalled, modestly, the risks that he himself had faced on the battlefields.

Alexander used inspiration to remind his troops of Cyrus the Younger and his Ten Thousand men, who had advanced into the Persian territory some seventy years before. That force, Alexander said, could not be compared with his force in strength and honor. They did not have the support of cavalry such as Thessalians, Boeotians, Peloponneses, Macedonians, and Thracians. They did not have archers or throwers other than a minor and improvised group from Crete and Rhodes. Even so, continued Alexander, Cyrus and the Ten Thousand had managed to beat the king of Persia at the entrance of Babylon[†] and to repulse the native forces

---

[†]Actually, the Greeks were initially victorious, but Cyrus was eventually killed in that battle (the Battle of Cunaxa). Then the soldier Xenophon led the heroic retreat of the Ten Thousand to the Black Sea.

that tried to block his march to the Black Sea.

Alexander also fostered revenge and hate against the enemy by recalling to his soldiers that the Persians had destroyed their temples, razed their cities, and dishonored the laws of gods and humans.

His speech animated the soldiers so much that they urged him to lead them against the *barbarians* without further delay. His officers, also inspired by the address, gathered to clasp his hand and to show their excitement. Before the battle, Alexander appealed to his people's religious faith by invoking the protection of the Greek gods. He had offered prayers and sacrifices to Thetis, Nereus, the Nereids, Poseidon, and Night. And he had revealed an optimistic prediction from the seer Aristander.

Alexander's eagerness to fight in the front line and to duel with the enemy's leader also showed up before that epic battle. An ancient mosaic of the battle eternalized the moment when Alexander eventually saw Darius for the first time. From a distance, Alexander saw his tall and fine-looking archrival defended by the finest Persian equestrians.

The Macedonians fighting next to Alexander were motivated by the actions of their leader, who—risking his life—had gotten into the line of Persian cavalry, while his counterpart remained hiding behind the protection of his best soldiers. The bravest Persian equestrians that managed to stay in Alexander's way were killed in front of Darius. Near the Persian king's chariot and before his incredulous eyes lay his most glorious generals. Among them were Atizyes, Rheomithres, and Sabaces, satrap of Egypt.

Fig. 9. Mosaic of the Battle of Issus: Alexander the Great (left) against Darius III (right). The mosaic was found in Pompeii and is now in the National Museum of Naples.[10]

During the pursuit of his Persian counterpart, Alexander continued to show courage, as he conducted the chase with just 1,000 cavalry while a massive number of Persians were in retreat.

Alexander's fighting ahead of his troops was typical. The king's presence in the frontlines played an important role in the outcome of battles. As time passed and Alexander kept winning battle after battle without a single loss, his mythical presence in the battlefronts, inspiring his soldiers and terrifying his enemies, became even more powerful.

Example beyond the Battlefields

Alexander spent a significant amount of his time in contact with commanders and soldiers of all ranks even when they were not at war. He visited his soldiers regularly in their working areas and talked to them. This sound habit, not common for a king, allowed him to get a firsthand opinion of his people's state of mind, to inspire them, and to build rapport. He believed that the more fluid the communication between a leader and his or her followers, the higher the level of trust and collaboration. Nevertheless, he kept a fine distinction between being accessible and still being the boss. He was one of them, but he was also their leader.

Alexander's fearlessness was also evident outside the battlefields. He was the type of leader who walked his talk. In fact, his actions were even more courageous and inspiring than his talks. As Afsaneh Nahavandi explains in *The Art and Science of Leadership*, "[Leaders] 'walk their talk,' whether is it through the self-sacrifice that they demand of their followers (for example, Gandhi and Nelson Mandela), or the self-control they demonstrate (for example, Martin Luther King, Jr.)."[11]

The king showed leadership and courage beyond the battlefields. By the end of 328 B.C. or the beginning of 327 B.C. the Macedonians were marching toward the region of Gazaba, unaware they were about to face a catastrophe. On the third day of their advance, lightning and thunder erupted and a freezing torrential rain hit them without mercy. The Macedonians tried to protect themselves with their shields, but soon their hands started to freeze.

Freezing and exhausted, they broke formation, making a desperate attempt to protect themselves against the weather. Some of them leaned against trees while others just lay down on the ground. As the bad weather persisted, the temperature had turned the ground into ice, so the soldiers lying there were freezing to death. Those under the trees were not fortunate either; the trees had served as protection from the hail, but the immobility of those soldiers decreased their body temperature so they became numb with cold, and they also were dying slowly.

As things got tough, Alexander became tougher. His pride helped him to hold up against the unexpected catastrophe. He walked around, helping the soldiers on the ground and encouraging them to fight against the cold. His soldiers, following their king's example, made an effort to stay in motion and cut down some trees to make fires and build shelters. The heat from the fire gradually warmed their limbs and saved most of them from dying.

This tragedy caused 2,000 deaths. Some soldiers were found frozen under the trees, looking as if they were still talking to other unfortunate casualties. The catastrophe, however, could have killed most of the soldiers had they remained immobile and not lighted fires. Alexander's leadership and example saved most of them.

Rolling up the Sleeves

Harry S. Truman said that a leader is a man who has the ability to get other people to do what they don't want to do, and like it.[12] Alexander's ability to work and endure hardships like a common soldier, and better, compelled his followers to adhere to his cause.

During the siege of the impregnable Tyre, Alexander fought and worked everywhere, sharing the hardships of his soldiers for seven straight months. After Byblus and Sidon surrendered to him (332 B.C.), Alexander proceeded toward the city of Tyre. On his way, representatives from the city approached him to say their government had decided to comply with any instructions of the Macedonian king. Tyre was an important, strategic port for the Persians, and they had anchored many of their ships in that city. Alexander expressed his gratitude to the representatives and asked them to return to Tyre and tell their people that he wanted to enter the city and offer sacrifice to Heracles—the Tyre Heracles, not the Argos one. He had learned this tactic of forcing a city to choose a side from his father.

The Tyrians were prepared to accede to Alexander's wishes, but they strongly opposed admitting any Macedonian, or even a Persian, to their city. They wanted to keep their neutrality because the result of the war between Alexander and Darius was still in doubt. Even though Alexander had defeated Darius in the Battle of Issus, Darius was gathering a massive army to fight Alexander again—this time in the plains.

Alexander became furious when he heard the news, as it was obvious to everyone that capturing Tyre would be impossible. Three hundred years before Alexander, King Nebakanezer of Babylon had besieged Tyre for thirteen consecutive years, but he failed to conquer it. The city was an island surrounded by two massive walls of big stones cemented together, approximately 150 feet high. The foundation of the outer wall was below sea level and just on the edge of the sea, which made it impossible for soldiers to land on the island.[13] In addition, the Persians ruled the sea and the Tyrian fleet was itself strong, making any attack by sea unimaginable.

In spite of all the difficulties ahead, Alexander was positive in dealing with his skeptical soldiers. He convinced his people of the need to take this strategically located city, and he added further encouragement with an interpretation of his dream, made by Aristander. In Alexander's dream, he was approaching the fortifications of Tyre, and Heracles invited him to enter the city. Aristander's interpretation was that Tyre would fall, but after long and hard work, as that was the case of Heracles' achievements.

Alexander planned to build a mole, a half mile long, from the land to the island. The Tyrians viewed this plan as absurd and it bewildered even his own soldiers. Alexander, however, did not back off and started the gigantic project. He was always at the scene of action sharing the hardships in person, working like any other soldier, giving words of encouragement to his people and reinforcement for the good work. The commanders, following his example, worked as hard as the soldiers did.

The problems started when the attackers reached deeper water, near the city walls. The construction was now within the Tyrians' missile range and the Macedonian men working in the mole were not dressed for battle, because they needed flexibility to work. In addition, the Tyrians took advantage of their clear supremacy at sea and sent steady raids against the mole, making the continuation of the engineering work almost impossible. To counter this, the Macedonians built two towers on the mole and equipped them with artillery to repel these raids. They also covered the towers with hides to provide some protection against the missiles thrown from the Tyrian walls.

The Tyrians soon came up with a bold new plan. They filled a boat with dry brushwood, timber, and other inflammable materials and waited for the right moment to send it against the mole. When the wind was favorable, they towed the boat with several triremes and directed it toward the mole. Before long, the mole and the two towers were burning, and the triremes, which had remained close to the mole, were shooting missiles at the towers to prevent the Macedonians from extinguishing the fire. Once the towers were burning, the Tyrian soldiers arrived from the city in several boats to set fire to the Macedonian war engines located on the mole.

Despite this setback, Alexander did not give up. He ordered his men to start the work again from scratch. This time the mole should be wider to allow more space for the war engines. Meanwhile, Alexander went in person to Sidon to assemble there all the combat ships that he had, with the intention of challenging the Tyrian superiority at sea. Alexander wisely used the propaganda of his victory at Issus against Darius to induce other cities to send him vessels. He knew that those cities had previously supported Persia because they had no other choice, but now that he had partially defeated Darius, the situation had changed. As a result, he received reinforcements of vessels from Phoenicia, Rhodes, Soli, Mallus, Lycia, Cyprus, and of course, Macedonia.

During the gathering of the fleet and the construction of the war engines, the natives of Mount Antilibanus in Arabia had killed some Macedonian men who were gathering timber for the towers. Alexander personally led an expedition to Mount Antilibanus and within ten days conquered the region. Afterward, he returned to Sidon and welcomed 4,000 Greek mercenaries who had arrived from the Peloponnese. Alexander then led the fleet toward Tyre. Surprised by the numerous ships of Cyprus and Phoenicia that had joined Alexander, the Tyrians decided not to risk a naval confrontation, and they instead barred the entrances to their seaport with ships.

The following day, Alexander blocked the city by sending the Cyprian fleet to control the northern harbor and the Phoenician fleet to the southern harbor. The brand-new war engines were placed on the mole and on the ships, and the assault began. The Tyrians responded to the attack with fire missiles, thrown from the crenellations near the mole; the rain of missiles plus some big stones that the Tyrians had pulled into the water stopped the Macedonians' advance again.

Alexander attempted to remove the stones and sent triremes to do the work, but the Tyrians kept sending divers to cut the anchor cables, so the ships could not remain steady. Then, Alexander replaced the cables of the anchors with stronger ropes to avert the divers' work. As the vessels gained steadiness, the Macedonians passed ropes around the stones and gradually lifted them away.

The Tyrians saw a turning point in the siege and decided to risk an attack against the Cyprian fleet that was blocking the northern harbor. They surprised the Cyprian vessels when most of the marines were engaged in various activities off board and sank some of their ships. As soon as Alexander was informed of the episode, he forewarned his fleet off the southern harbor about the threat of a similar Tyrian maneuver in that area. Then, he sailed to the northern harbor to fight the Tyrian fleet with triremes and quinqueremes (galleys having five benches of oars) . When the Tyrians in the crenellations saw Alexander in person leading the fleet, they tried to warn their vessels, but the Tyrian crews saw their enemies too late and did not have time to reach the harbor. As a result, Alexander's ships violently struck most of their vessels, and the Tyrians had to swim to save their lives.

Now that he had damaged the Persian fleet, Alexander found it easier to start using the siege engines. He positioned them on the south side because he noticed that the wall there was weaker than near the mole. He was in person on the tallest siege engine, where his bright armor and royal insignia inspired his soldiers, but his blazing presence also made him a clear target for the Tyrian missiles. The siege engine he had climbed was almost at the edge of the city walls. And from there, Alexander gave a spectacular lesson in courage to his people by fighting and killing many defenders—both with his spear and in hand-to-hand combat.

After a time, part of the city wall began to collapse, and finally the Macedonians made a small breach in the wall. The breach, however, was still too small to force an entrance, and the Tyrians easily repelled the attempts. Alexander's words of encouragement inspired his soldiers once more.

After three days, when the weather was favorable, Alexander used the ship's artillery to damage the city walls. Meanwhile, he sent other vessels to sail around the island, threatening attacks at several points, and therefore diverting the attention of Tyrians. When the breach was bigger, he sent two ships to place gangways across the breach. Alexander was in one of these ships, ready to invade the city.

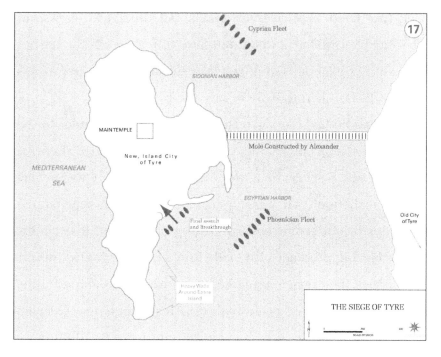

Fig. 10. Courtesy of the Department of History, United States Military Academy.

Soon the Macedonian battalion of the Guards was pressing into the hole, and Alexander himself was fighting with them, encouraging his soldiers every time he noticed the slightest sign of doubt on their faces. A spear killed one of the leaders of the attack, Admetus, but the group that Alexander was leading soon gained ground against the Tyrian defenders. Subsequently, Alexander got control of the breach and some of the towers near it. Most of the Tyrian defenders retreated from the walls to fight the Macedonians at the holy place of Agenor, founder of Tyre, but soon their fight became hopeless against the fierce attack of Alexander and the Guards. In the meantime, the attackers' fleet had successfully overcome the defensive booms, and now they were in control of the harbors and the town.

The conquest of Tyre, one of the most incredible achievements of any army, was finally over after seven long and exhausting months. Alexander had seized the city in an unimaginable way, even by today's standards. During this unrelenting siege, the Tyrians lost 8,000 soldiers and the Macedonians 400. Only the Tyrians who found refuge in Heracles' temple—where Alexander finally made his sacrifice—received their freedom. The rest, 30,000 people, were sold into slavery. Alexander had secured an extraordinary victory against a city that was considered impregnable, and he had sent a message to other cities in the world: *He would fight for as long as it took to achieve his goals.*

For this victory to happen, it was essential that the soldiers went the extra mile every day of the siege; he had led the way by working and fighting among them—not as a king, but as a common soldier.

From his teenage years, Alexander had frequently performed tasks of a common soldier. Throughout his campaigns, in plenty of situations, the king showed his eagerness to work in affairs that others considered tasks of common soldiers or support men. During the campaign against the Uxians, for instance, in autumn of 331 B.C., Alexander left his camp by the night shift, crossed a valley at dawn, and cut wood to make shelters and protect the men who were working at the siege engines from the missiles thrown from the city.

A few months after that episode, he and his soldiers were engaged in a long and painful chase of Darius. After eleven days, the Macedonians were so exhausted and thirsty that most of them wanted to quit the grueling pursuit. During a stop, some soldiers who had brought water from a distant river saw Alexander almost choked with thirst. The soldiers filled a helmet with water and offered it to the king.

Alexander asked them to whom they were carrying that water, and they responded that it was for their sons who were in Alexander's column. Alexander took the helmet, but when he looked around and saw all the people eagerly desirous for a sip of water, he gave back the helmet without drinking a drop of water. He said he could not drink alone, and it was impossible to share that little with everyone. He went on and told them to hurry and give their sons what they had brought for them.

This fairness and self-control was so well received by the troops that they disregarded their previous desire to give up the pursuit, and instead, they asked Alexander to lead them toward Darius.

Pushing the Limits

"Never forget," said the Prussian general and military strategist Karl von Clausewitz (1780-1831), "that no military leader has ever become great without audacity."[14] Martin Luther King, Jr., said that a man who won't die for something is not fit to live.[15] Alexander was the kind of man who would die for his goals. What is more, his disregard for death terrified his enemies, and his soldiers loved that.

After the successful siege of Tyre, Alexander advanced toward Egypt according to the plan he had shared with his commanders before attacking Tyre. All the Syrian Palestine except Gaza had surrendered to him. Batis, governor of Gaza, was loyal to his king and confident in the apparent invulnerability of his city. Gaza was a big town located on top of a mound, protected by a robust wall and surrounded by deep sand, which made it difficult for siege engines to attack it. In addition, Batis had recruited an important number of Arab mercenaries to protect the city.

Alexander's engineers advised him that the height of the mound where the city was located made it impossible to attack the town, but Alexander believed that the greater the obstacle, the more essential it was to overcome it. He believed a victory beyond realistic expectation would have a significant impact on the self-esteem of his enemies, while a failure would represent a similarly important setback to his reputation. Therefore, he ordered his people to prepare for the siege, assemble the war engines, circle the city with a wall, and place the engines on it. The southern side of the wall seemed to be more vulnerable than the rest of it, so, Alexander concentrated the work in that area. After the earthwork had reached enough height, the siege engines were placed upon it.

As usual, Alexander offered sacrifices before starting the attack; during the ceremony, a crow flying over the place happened to drop a clod that landed on the king's head. When Alexander asked the prophet Aristander, who enjoyed great credibility, about the meaning of the omen, Aristander said that Gaza would be taken; but the king would be in danger and should not attack that same day. Alexander, discontentedly, followed the soothsayer's advice and ordered a retreat.

This retreat gave a boost to the defenders as they thought the Macedonians and their allies had had second thoughts about the attack. Thus, the Arab soldiers made a raid on the Macedonians to burn the siege engines, and they nearly succeeded in pushing the Macedonians back down the bulwark. At the noise and the sight of his troops facing a serious attack, Alexander rushed to fight on the front line.

An enemy soldier who claimed to be a deserter prostrated himself before Alexander, and the king received him among his men; but the false deserter suddenly took a sword he had hidden behind his shield and thrust at Alexander's neck. The king made a small swift movement to the side, averted the strike, and cut off the attacker's hand with his sword.

Alexander had been very close to death, but the danger to his life did not end there. He was still fighting at the head of his troops when a missile thrown from a catapult hit him. The missile pierced his corselet and stuck in his shoulder until his physician, Philip, removed it and placed a bandage on the wound. Alexander was bleeding considerably, but he remained standing for a long time. However, when the blood began to flow more profusely, he started to faint. Then, a soldier near the king grabbed him and took him to the camp.

Alexander ordered his men to raise the earthwork and brought into action the artillery that had been helpful in the siege of Tyre. The defenders built additional defenses, but the Macedonian towers were still higher than the walls and able to rain missiles into the city of Gaza. Soon, the artillery work of the attackers plus the unnoticed tunnels dug under the wall started to cause serious damage to it, until finally the wall collapsed. Before his injury had completely healed, Alexander led the attack of his infantry again. Once again a missile struck him, this time on the leg; but he held himself up with a spear and kept fighting in the front line with increased rage.

The soldiers of Gaza fought bravely to their deaths; their women and children were enslaved. Repeating what he had read in *The Iliad*, Alexander dragged Batis around the city with his war chariot, as Achilles had done with Hector. The king ended this battle physically injured, but his reputation as warrior and leader had increased significantly.

Although Alexander's recurring presence at the head of his troops clearly boosted the confidence and energy of his people, it also had a negative side. The king's constant exposure to such serious risks almost got him killed many times. Every time he was wounded, his soldiers responded with additional rage and violence against the enemies, but his opponents were also encouraged by the occasional misstep of the invincible Macedonian.

When the Macedonians were besieging Cyropolis in the year 329 B.C., Alexander had decided—initially—to show mercy to the city, but the obstinate resistance of the town made him change his mind. He became very angry and eventually ordered his troops to pillage Cyropolis. Notwithstanding, the city continued to offer great resistance to the attack; and during this very tough siege, Alexander lost some of his best soldiers and faced great danger himself. A stone hit his neck, causing such serious damage that he fell unconscious on the ground. At first, his army thought he was dead and wept for him, but they continued to fight bravely. Even before he fully recovered, Alexander increased the siege. He made a large hole through the city walls. When the defenses of Cyropolis were finally defeated, the Macedonian king ordered the destruction of the city.

By the beginning of the year 326 B.C., Alexander approached the rock of Aornos, which, according to legend, even Heracles had failed to seize. This impressive rock, steep on every side, had a height of about 8,000 feet and a circumference of 25 miles. Driven by the legend of Heracles and the challenge of the endeavor, Alexander was eager to capture Aornos.

He ordered his men to fill the gaps on the far side of the rock with tree trunks, and again, he became the first to start working in the woods while all his people followed the example. Who could complain about work that the king himself was undertaking faster and better than most of his subordinates? The climbing started as soon as the job was finished.

Initially, the attackers decided that Alexander would not participate in the rock climbing because the operation was very dangerous and required special skills, but Alexander could not resist the temptation to take the lead. So he was, in fact, the first to climb up the steep cliff. Watching the king taking the lead, no Macedonian waited. The ascension proved extremely difficult and claimed many lives. To make things worse, the Indians of Aornos started to throw missiles and boulders at the Macedonians, killing additional soldiers and spreading terror among the survivors.

Alexander and Charus managed to keep climbing and were the first to engage in hand-to-hand fighting with the Indians, who also kept throwing missiles at the attackers from higher ground. The king became the target of several weapons and eventually fell after receiving several injuries. Charus, seeing his friend on the ground, charged furiously against the defenders; but after killing some of them, he was finally killed.[‡]

Given the critical situation, Alexander had to give up ground, but he did not abandon the siege. He persisted in sending company after company up the cliff, replacing exhausted units with fresh ones. Catapults and siege machines supported the troops' work, with Alexander personally supervising the work and pushing his people. After three days of resistance, the Indians ran

---

[‡]Version of historian Quintus Curtius Rufus

away under cover of night. While they were escaping, however, Alexander's soldiers killed a large number of them.

Alexander came out victorious against an enemy that had frustrated Heracles himself—according to the legend. This remarkable victory—more over extreme topography than over a powerful army—again showed the king fighting and working as the first warrior of his army.

Alexander's most dangerous adventure was his campaign against the city of the Mallians, who had the reputation of being the most courageous warriors in all of India. The attack began by the year 325 B.C. with Alexander leading one unit and Perdicas another. Surprisingly, the Indians did not offer resistance outside the fortress, but they placed all their men within the inner walls.

Alexander ordered his men to place the ladders in position to climb those walls. But since his soldiers were not fast enough to meet his expectations, he grabbed a ladder himself, leaned it against the wall, and started to climb up before anyone else. He was the first one to reach the top of the wall, and he initially killed some Indians while forcing others to retreat into the fort. His soldiers, however, were not able to reach him because of the persistent rain of missiles thrown from the city; therefore, the king stayed alone, at the top of the narrow wall.

Although no Mallian dared to approach him after he killed the first defenders, Alexander, with his armor and courage announcing who he was, became the target of missiles thrown from every tower near him. He managed to resist temporarily by using his shield to stop the missiles.

Deeply concerned about their leader staying alone at the mercy of the enemy, the Macedonians made another effort to climb the ladders, despite the rain of missiles. Unfortunately for their king, they overcharged the ladders and broke them, sending every man to the ground and depriving Alexander of his last hope for help. As a result, Alexander remained hopeless and isolated in front of a well-armed enemy.

Instead of accepting a sure death by staying at the top of he wall, Alexander leaped down into the city, with such good fortune and equilibrium that he landed on his feet. Alexander leaned against a tree near the city wall to avoid being surrounded, and he used his shield to protect himself against the missiles. First, some defenders rushed toward him, but he killed them. Next, two commanders attacked him. He killed one of them, and the other he forced to retreat. After that, no other Indian dared to fight him hand-to-hand. Alexander's widespread fame, in addition to his courageous and obstinate defense, certainly influenced the Indians at that moment.

Nevertheless, the defenders had formed a semicircle and attacked him at long range with all kinds of missiles. Alexander managed to stop the missiles with his shield for a while, but eventually a large arrow passed through his body armor, entered his body above the breast, and pierced his lung. The impact was so strong that it pushed him backward and caused him to drop his weapon. With a lung pierced, and hemorrhaging, Alexander did not have enough strength to remove the arrow. Then the same man who had wounded him, seeing Alexander almost dead, rushed toward him to kill him. In his eagerness, the Indian left one side unguarded, and the king capitalized on that mistake by killing his enemy.

Alexander challenged the rest of his enemies for a moment, but soon he lost all his strength, first kneeling, and then falling over his shield. By then, Peucestas, Abreas, and Leonnatus, who had climbed the ladders before they broke and had forced out the Indians in other parts of the town, arrived to help their king. Peucestas and Leonnatus stood in front of Alexander protecting him with their shields and their own bodies. Meanwhile, more Indians from other parts of the city arrived, as they had learned that the king himself was inside the fortress. Abreas was the first one to die, receiving a wound in the face after having fought with courage. Peucestas and Leonnatus were seriously wounded, the first losing his shield, and the second falling almost dead at Alexander's feet.

By that time, a few Macedonian soldiers had finally succeeded in climbing the walls, using any device that they found handy. They had seen their king leap down into the city, and now, watching him lying on the ground, they thought he was dead. A few soldiers rushed to cover Alexander's body with their shields, and the rest engaged in a violent fight against the Indians. The remaining Macedonian troops had made a hole in the wall and opened the gate of the city. As soon as they broke in, a mass butchering began, and the Macedonian rage did not discriminate among men, women, and children.

A group of soldiers carried Alexander on his shield to the camp. Back in his tent, the doctors cut the arrow, leaving the head inside his body; they were afraid to take out the rest because it could damage a vital organ during the removal. Furthermore, there was a very good chance that Alexander would bleed even more and die during the operation. The physicians feared for their own fate in the event of Alexander's death.

The king perceived the dilemma and encouraged the best of them, Critobulus, to go ahead and free him from that terrible pain, whatever the outcome would be. Critobulus then had no alternative. He made the wound larger and pulled out the head of the arrow. But as feared, the hemorrhage increased, and Alexander soon fainted. Grief and desperation spread among his soldiers, who believed him dead, as they considered that their life depended on his. Who would lead them back home now? Who would care for them? Who would inspire them during the battles and perils?

Luckily for everyone, especially for Critobulus, the hemorrhage eventually stopped, and Alexander gradually recovered consciousness. Even after several days, however, he remained very weak, and his wound was still unhealed. Rumors of his death had spread among his enemies, and his soldiers had doubts about his chances to recover fully. Given this scenario, the king thought it was essential for him to appear in front of his people to prevent a discipline problem among his soldiers and a revolt among his defeated enemies. Thus, he asked to be carried to the river Hydraotes, and then he proceeded downstream toward the camp where most of his troops were.

Upon arriving at the camp, Alexander raised his hand from the boat, and at once, his soldiers responded with cries of relief and happiness. He asked to be taken to the shore so all the soldiers could see him. Then his Guards brought him a stretcher, but he surprised everyone by asking for his horse instead. The cheers of his people were even louder when they saw the king mounting his horse. He advanced toward his tent and dismounted there. Then everyone walked toward him to touch his hand, his clothes, or even his knees. Such was the kind of inspiration that this young leader triggered among his people—the young and the old, the lowest and the highest in rank.

The Macedonians and their allies had good reasons to celebrate Alexander's recovery. They had advanced beyond the Euphrates River, and they thought that if something happened to their king they would remain isolated among their enemies. Since no heir to Alexander's throne had been chosen, everyone would try to appropriate the king's power.

Craterus' speech during those days summarized the dichotomy of the Macedonians' sentiment:

No matter how powerful an army unite against us from the world over; no matter though it fill the entire earth with arms and men or pave the seas over with ships or bring strange monsters against us—you will make us invincible. But which of the gods can guarantee that this mainstay, this star of Macedon will long continue

when you are so ready to expose yourself to obvious danger, un-
aware that you draw the lives of so many of your fellow citizens
into disaster? Who wants to survive you? Who is able to? Follow-
ing your authority and your command we have reached a place
from which returning home without your leadership is impossible
for any of us.[16]

Projecting Confidence

Projecting confidence sometimes becomes a self-fulfilling prophecy. In the book *The Art and Science of Leadership,*[17] Afsaneh Nahavandi explains that the more confident the leader, the more motivated the followers who then wholeheartedly carry out the leader's wishes. Such motivation and hard work, says Nahavandi, increase the chances of success, which provides proof of the leader's righteousness. "A leader," as Napoleon Bonaparte has said, "is a dealer in hope."[18]

As previously mentioned in this book, Alexander was very perceptive about the feelings of his people and was prompt to encourage them every time he noticed their anxiety. He motivated his soldiers with precise and encouraging words and actions—during or before a battle—and his supreme confidence became evident and contagious in rough situations. The harder the circumstances, the tougher he became. Furthermore, he urged his generals to motivate their own units, so those generals empowered their soldiers.

While advancing to meet Darius' army at Gaugamela, during September of the year 331 B.C., Alexander noticed that panic had spread among his soldiers; therefore, he stopped the march, ordered the troops to rest, and prepared to address them. Alexander spoke to them with encouraging words and explained to them that the enemy was still far away from them. Only when he judged that his people had recovered their confidence did he order them to pick up their arms and resume the advance.

On the morning of the battle, Alexander was still sleeping when the sun rose, so Parmenio entered his tent and awakened him. Parmenio was surprised at his deep and sound sleep before such a decisive event. Alexander explained to him that he was actually pleased, because Darius, after burning the land before them, trying to starve them by lack of supplies, had finally decided to fight. "Now that he [Darius] is preparing to decide the issue in battle, what do I have to fear?"[19] the king asked.

Such confidence, whether it was real or pretended, had a positive effect on his soldiers. The king, the leader, supposedly knows more and has more information than his followers; therefore, if he is confident the rest will be. As Warren Bennis and Burt Nanus explained in their book *Leaders: Strategies for Taking Charge*,[20] "True leaders have an uncanny way of enrolling people in their vision through their optimism—sometimes unwarranted optimism."

The opposite is also true. Followers' morale seriously diminishes, and they become uncertain when they smell doubt or weakness in the leader.

During the heat of this epic battle, Alexander showed one more time his virtues as a leader. Together with his Companions, he was on the spot ready to support his soldiers when they needed it the most. Fighting visibly in the front line, his presence boosted the adrenaline of his people and caused fear in the enemy's lines. He reproached and encouraged Aretes and his unit when they, crushed by the Bactrian units that Darius had sent against them, retreated to the position where Alexander was. Their confidence restored, Alexander ordered them to charge the enemy one more time.

Alexander normally projected a confident image of himself, but during battles and other dangerous situations, that self-confidence was most obvious. Fighting furiously hand to hand at the head of his troops, Alexander showed a different attitude than most of his opponents.

Chapter VII

Managing Reputation

"Lose money for the firm, and I will be understanding; lose a shred of reputation for the firm, and I will be ruthless."[1]

Warren Buffett

"CHARISMATIC LEADERS," SAYS Afsaneh Nahavandi,[2] "are masterful impression managers." Alexander was a charismatic leader who created, through time, a formidable emotional impact on his followers. Truly enthusiastic about his revolutionary vision and ideas, he surrounded himself with symbols that built his image as a role model. In turn, his personal magnetism and reputation helped him to increase his *referent power.*

His approach was particularly useful for those times, since the Greeks had a strong belief in prophecy and divine salvation.

Most charismatic leaders emerge during times of crisis that spur major changes. The crisis in Macedonia was the question of succession to Philip's throne and the negative consequences that this situation had on Macedonians' adversaries.

Not all good leaders, however, are charismatic. Harry Truman is a good example of a non-charismatic leader who, in spite of that, had a profound impact on the history of the United States.

The Power of Reputation

Solomon, the son of David, king of Israel, held that a good name is rather to be chosen than great riches.[3] Alexander was well aware of the importance of reputation. He knew that his prestige helped him boost his power, "for reputation determines military success, and often even a false belief has accomplished as much as the truth."[4] Alexander masterfully managed his image. He always considered the impact that his decisions would have on his enemies and his own people. He designed his messages carefully and presented himself as a role model for his followers. Similar to Martin Luther King, Jr., Alexander used nonverbal expressions to reinforce his messages. The perceptions he created helped him to promote his cause, and in some cases, they became a self-fulfilling prophecy.

Jeffrey Pfeffer, writing about the interrelation of reputation, performance, and position, has noted that position and reputation are sources of power, in part, because of what they imply about the individual's ability to perform his or her job effectively.[5]

Reputation is particularly important during the first days of a person as a leader of a particular group. The first impression a leader makes on his or her followers, peers, and enemies is crucial, and may determine the person's future as the group's leader. He or she has only one chance to make a good first impression.

When Alexander inherited the throne from his father Philip, he knew that he had to capitalize on his chance quickly to build and consolidate a power base. Many Macedonians, and even more Greeks, challenged his legitimacy as king of Macedonia. Some Greeks even considered him a barbarian. Alexander was fully aware that others would closely and minutely examine his initial acts and decisions. Therefore, he paid special attention to his public appearances; every public act from speeches to religious participation had an objective.

Early in his campaign in Asia Minor, during the siege of Miletus, Alexander decided not to engage in a naval combat against the Persians, because he acknowledged that his strength was on the land, not at sea. Not only was the Persian fleet much larger than its counterpart (400 Persian vessels versus 160 Greek), Alexander was not expert in sea battles. The king did not want to risk his early reputation of invincibility in a naval fight where he would have little control over the outcome.

Building Historical Glamour

Alexander represented the kind of leader that every soldier would like to have: courageous, determined, and undefeated. His idea that nothing was impossible for him, supported by a relentless record of achievements, enhanced his mystique and even induced some to worship him as a god during his own time and for centuries after his death.

Before starting his campaign in Asia, Alexander crossed the Hellespont and arrived at the ruins of Troy by the year 334 B.C. He was especially interested in visiting the gravestone of his ancestor Achilles and honoring him. He also praised the goddess Athena, offered his own shield to her, and took the strongest shield from the temple as a symbol of divine protection. The purpose of the expedition to Troy was to develop Alexander's glamour.

Alexander created a mystical image around his person. The Macedonians had a remarkable victory in the siege of Gaza during September-October 332 B.C. He punished Batis, the leader in the defense of the city, by having Batis' feet tied with leather strips and the strips secured to the back of Alexander's chariot. Then Alexander dragged Batis around the city as the Homeric hero Achilles had done.

Some talented actors maintain that dressing is a very important part of acting. Alexander dressed like a Homeric hero during battles. From his shiny silver helmet, to his double thick aegis, to his remarkably lightweight but strong sword, to his special woven shirt, and to his intimidating horse, the king projected a magnificent and glamorous image.

He liked to add glamour by comparing his troops with the Ten Thousand of Cyrus the Younger and Xenophon. According to Alexander, he and his people were far better than their predecessors were. They were the liberators of the world, and one glorious day they would cross the boundaries established by Heracles and conquer the entire human race.

He increased his fame by having silver coins struck with his face on them as his father Philip had done. These coins followed the standard established by Athens and followed by other cities. In this way, Greece and the newly added territories would be linked by a common currency: the coin of Alexander. The use of symbols to underscore historical moments, like ordering the trumpets to sound at the beginning of important events, was a trademark of Alexander's marketing campaign.

Fig. 11. Coin of Alexander the Great (4th century B.C.).[6]

His unprecedented record of achievements eventually found the king with far more glories than any other hero—either real or mythological. As time passed, Alexander surpassed first his father Philip II of Macedon, then Cyrus the Younger and Xenophon, then Achilles, and finally Heracles. The historical glamour of Alexander III of Macedonia became an example for many other leaders, including Roman emperors and Napoleon.

Perception Influences Reality

Alexander's first battle in Asian territory happened around April-June 334 B.C. at the Granicus River. One of the reasons why Alexander decided to cross the river and attack his opponents the same afternoon he arrived there was his concern for the Persians' perception about him and his army. He did not want to damage his army's reputation for courage by stopping before a river like Granicus, when he had already crossed the Hellespont—although there were no enemies to fight at the Hellespont.

He did not want the Persians to think he was doubtful or afraid of them; neither did he want his people to have that perception. In his own words, "Such hesitancy would be unworthy of the fighting fame of our people and of my own promptitude in the face of danger. Without doubt it would give the Persians added confidence; nothing has yet happened to them to cause them alarm, and they would begin to think they were as good soldiers as we are."[7] Alexander made sure that all his high commanders, including Parmenio, who opposed his idea, heard his bold statement.

During that battle, Alexander was fighting everywhere with the white crest of his helmet announcing his presence at the head of the elite squad.

To gain the support of Greece, Athens in particular, he sent 300 Persian armors to share his victory with the Hellenics. The armors he sent had the following inscription: "Alexander, son of Philip, and the Greeks, except the Spartan, captured this prize from the Asian barbarians."[8] The inscription carried a smart message. First, it was a warning to the rebellious Spartans. Second, it aimed to gain the support of the Greeks by calling the Persians *barbarians,* a Hellenic term to refer to non-Greeks. Alexander ordered the armors to be placed in Athena's temple, promoting the idea that his campaign was, in fact, a Hellenic crusade.

Alexander created the image that he was fighting to free subjugated nations. He convinced Macedonians first, and Greeks later, that he was crusading to liberate the Greek cities of Asia Minor under enemy control and to punish the Persians for their past behavior. After he gained control over Asia Minor, Alexander created the perception that he was the modern liberator of all the cities under Persian dominion, beyond Asia Minor.

Alexander realized that some cities had supported Persia by necessity rather than choice. By respecting each nation's religion and traditions, and by sometimes imposing fewer taxes than the Great King Darius had, he gained the favor and respect of many of the cities he conquered. Furthermore, Alexander embraced new cultures, honored local gods and heroes, and occasionally used local garments. He married spouses from other countries and encouraged his people to do the same.

Most business leaders are becoming increasingly aware of the importance that public perception has in contemporary corporate settings. Some of those leaders have successfully used methods that are similar to Alexander's techniques. Other business leaders, however, have hard times managing their public image.

When Jack Welch retired from General Electric (GE) in 2001, he had to choose a successor between his two protégé: Jeffrey Immelt and Bob Nardelli. Jack Welch chose the first. Since then to 2006, Mr. Immelt led GE and Mr. Nardelli became the CEO of Home Depot. Also since then to 2006, neither of these two CEOs earned money for shareholders. In fact, they decreased shareholders' value. Yet, the public perception of these two high-profile leaders was quite different.

Mr. Immelt, a tall and smooth graduate of Dartmouth and Harvard, was ranked as one of the world's *Best CEOs* by Barron's. He led the *Most Admired Company* (according to Fortune) and one of the two *Most Respected Companies* (according to *Financial Times*). Meanwhile, the media and shareholders criticized regularly Mr. Nardelli, a short and brusque CEO with no Ivy League degrees. And Mr. Nardelli had a much harder job with Home Depot than Mr. Immelt with GE—a company in a very good shape.

Jeff Immelt was much more sensitive to his public image. As the *Wall Street Journal* reported, "Mr. Immelt has worked to appease corporate critics. He made his company's operations more transparent, reached out to a wide range of 'stakeholders,' emphasized good corporate 'citizenship' and even took the extraordinary step of adopting self-imposed limits on GE's greenhouse-gas emissions, earning kudos from environmentalists. Perhaps most importantly, he asked his board to forgo his cash bonus and give him 'performance shares,' which only pay if he meets his targets—though skeptics say those targets aren't that hard to meet. Mr. Nardelli took a very different approach. On at least three occasions, when the game was going against him, he and his board tried to alter the rules. With shareholder returns in the dumps, they changed his incentive pay from a formula based on shareholder returns to one based on earnings per share. With store sales down, they decided to stop disclosing Home Depot's same-store sales. And when union shareholders went on the attack, they held a sham annual meeting, with no directors present and strict time limits on statements from the floor."[9]

"How Mr. Immelt turned poor performance into a badge of honor while Mr. Nardelli turned it into a badge of shame speaks volumes about the post-Enron world of business. Success and failure are no longer a simple matter of shareholder returns. For better or worse, it is a much more public game, involving a wide range of constituencies and requiring the skills of a politician,"[10] Alan Murray of *The Wall Street Journal* summarized.

Business leaders—like other leaders—must remain watchful of public perception. Because people do not react to reality, they react to their perception of it. And in the end, perception influences reality and tends to become a self-fulfilling prophecy.

Influencing Adversaries

Alexander believed that reputation, whether true or false, had a strong influence on military achievements, so he took every opportunity to upset his enemies. At the same time, he was very careful to protect his own reputation. He would make use of apparently minor symbols, actions, and speeches to undermine his enemies' morale.

In a typical lecture to his officers, he would instruct them that their men should move forward in complete silence and watch the best moment for a vigorous shout. Then, they should roar their typical war cry and fill their enemies' hearts with terror.

The capture of the Sogdian Rock is a good example of Alexander's ability to impress his enemies and capitalize on it. By the year 327 B.C., Arimazes had been defending the Sogdian Rock with approximately 30,000 soldiers for two years. The rock had precipitous sides, and reaching the top meant taking a narrow path that the defenders occupied. Knowing that seizing the rock would be extremely difficult, if possible at all, and would take a long time, Alexander sent an ambassador—Cophes—to ask for Arimazes' capitulation. As expected, Arimazes was very confident about the difficulties of the terrain and his defense of it, so he rejected the offer. What's more, he made disdainful comments and asked whether Alexander's soldiers could fly. Alexander became furious when he heard about the *barbarian insolence*, and he took it as a personal insult.

He called his commanders and asked them to send him the best mountain climbers available in their units. Afterward, he received the young men and gave them one of his touching speeches, emphasizing that nature had placed nothing so high that it could not be overcome by guts. He added a handsome monetary incentive for those who reached the top first. The enthusiasm of the young climbers was impressive. Alexander instructed the selected soldiers to find any alternative way to climb, other than the path protected by the Sogdians, while he diverted the Sogdians' attention with tactical maneuvers of his troops.

Each climber took supplies for two days, a sword, and a spear. The climb proved to be deadly difficult. Many men fell, spreading terror among those who remained alive. Despite the numerous difficulties, they managed to reach the top of the mountain. The next morning, they placed cloths on their spears to signal their arrival at the summit. As soon as Alexander saw the signal, initially unclear due to the conditions of the sky, he sent Cophes again to ask for the Sogdians' surrender. In the event of a refusal, the most likely scenario, Alexander instructed Cophes to show the Sogdians the soldiers who had reached the top of the mountain.

Cophes did as planned, and Arimazes refused the proposal, adding comments more rebellious and disrespectful than before. Then Cophes took Arimazes' hand and asked him to go with him outside the cave, where he showed Arimazes Alexander's soldiers on the top of mountain. He said that Alexander's soldiers *did* have wings. At that precise moment, the Macedonian armies at the camp blasted their trumpets and roared.

This theatrical performance terrified the Sogdians so much that they did not stop to think how many enemies could had made it to the top—a small number, in fact. Cophes left them; and the Sogdians, despairing, went after him sending thirty chieftains to negotiate the terms of their capitulation. Alexander, furious at Arimazes' arrogance, did not accept any conditions for the capitulation. Even Arimazes' visit to Alexander, together with his family and other nobles, did not calm the king, who at last ordered them to be crucified.

Alexander's growing fame, in addition to his other qualities, helped him during difficult circumstances. His reputation, for instance, influenced the Mallians who did not dare to fight him hand to hand after he killed some of them when he was isolated inside their city.

Celebrating and Publicizing Victories

Alexander was almost as good at publicizing his victories as he was at winning them. Unless the urgency of the situation required otherwise, he would celebrate his victories and share those special moments with his people. He also made sure that his fellow citizens, as well as his previous, current, and potential opponents became aware of his latest achievements. His soldiers on leave, for example, would broadcast his most recent victories upon their return to their native cities, reinforcing his reputation and motivating younger soldiers to join the invincible army of Alexander.

To celebrate and share victories with his people, Alexander typically performed three different types of activities. First, he offered sacrifices to Greek gods, and at times to local gods, in gratitude for their help in his campaigns. Second, he held ceremonial parades of all his troops, wearing battle equipment to boost their pride and self-confidence and to prolong the cheerful post-victory spirit. When possible, the fleet would also participate in this event. Third, he organized contests: athletic games, music and verse competitions, and torch races.

Often, the Macedonians' victories were against the terrain rather than the enemy, like the capture of Aornos and of the Sogdian Rock. Alexander celebrated those victories like any other conquest even though they were not so much military achievements.

Celebrating successes was also a way of making winning moments more memorable. Eventually, Alexander would go back to those glorious memories during or before critical events to cheer his people and himself. Right before battles, for instance, he would proudly look at his soldiers and remind them of their previous achievements.

The king acknowledged the perils ahead when communicating with his soldiers, but he talked about the challenges with a positive bias. He typically diminished the importance of his current adversaries, and at the same time he boosted his people's morale—partially by emphasizing the importance of the opponents that he had already defeated.

Publicizing victories and achievements tends to have a snowball effect. More often than not, it increases the winner's confidence and undermines his adversaries' morale. Alexander aimed to spread the news of his accomplishments to influence undecided key players. And by doing so, he persuaded some cities to join him rather than oppose him. During the arduous siege of Tyre, for instance, he succeeded in getting naval support from Tyre's neighbor cities.

The news that the Macedonian king had defeated Darius at Issus and now controlled the entire Phoenicia encouraged some of these cities, particularly Cyprus, to support Alexander. He knew that those cities had previously used their naval force to support the Great King by necessity rather than preference, so he convinced them that the power allocation was shifting and pushed them to end their neutrality and to choose a side. Their decision favored the rising star of Alexander.

Divine Fortune

Generally, countries of the ancient world tended to be very religious and superstitious. Macedonia was not an exception. Partly because he was a religious person, and partly to capitalize on people's beliefs, Alexander made every possible effort to align himself with these beliefs. His mother Olympia often claimed Alexander was the son of the Greek god. In addition, a few oracles had interpreted deities' words as a revelation of Alexander's divine origin.

Whether Alexander believed those stories or not, he did not deny them. Instead, he took advantage of the situation to magnify his importance in the eyes of his soldiers and enemies. He put questions to the oracles in Greece and Egypt and received—or so he said—encouraging answers. The dissemination of those divine endorsements increased the hope and confidence of his tired and sometimes doubtful soldiers. Julius Cesar later copied this strategy and tried to convince his troops of his descent form Venus—the Roman goddess of love and beauty equivalent to the Greek goddess Aphrodite.

The Macedonian king liked to attribute his good fortune to the assistance of the gods; he would claim that divine favor, rather than good luck, backed him.

To strengthen his alleged bonds with the gods and get their favor, Alexander did not miss any opportunity to offer them sacrifices, presents, parades, and other solemn symbols. Zeus, Heracles, Athena, and Artemis were among his favorites. Before important events, especially battles, the prophet Aristander would typically lead Alexander in prayer while the king requested the assistance of the gods. Beyond the religious significance, these rites proved very efficient in calming the fears of his troops.

After a battle was finished, Alexander did not forget to thank the gods who had supposedly helped him win. After all, he would need their assistance for the next battle. Subsequent to the siege of Tyre, for instance, he offered solemn sacrifices to Heracles and dedicated a symbol of his victory him, in this case, a Tyrian ship captured during a naval combat. Another emblem of this laborious conquest, the part of a siege engine used to make a breach in the Tyrian walls, was presented to the temple.

Some of Alexander's commanders did not like his assertion that he was the son of Zeus, and much less, the solemn adoration the Persians offered him after he conquered them. He based his justifications on the gods' oracular responses and on the advantages that a title of son of Zeus would probably have in front of his enemies. In spite of the discontent of some Macedonians and Greeks, his divine pretensions appeared to pay off in time, as some of his enemies feared him as a god. Even after his demise, some cities continued to worship Alexander as a god for a long time—in a few cases, centuries.

Chapter VIII

Conquering the People

"Possession achieved by the sword is not of long duration, but grati-tude for kindness shown is everlasting." Alexander[1]

Early Magnanimity

THE INITIAL YEARS of Alexander's rule showed him as a mag-nanimous and generous leader who gradually gained the sympathy of most Macedonians, many Greeks and Egyptians, and some Asians. As Lao-tzu said, "To lead, one must follow."[2] The Macedonians were the first to fall in love with the young king, in part because of the hardships he faced at a young age and the courage he showed in overcoming them. The bravery he revealed at the Battle of Chaeronea, where he helped his father defeat the Athenians and Thebans, the obstacles and humiliations he surmounted to access the Macedonian throne after his father's murder, and his early generosity all helped him to conquer the hearts of his fellow citizens.

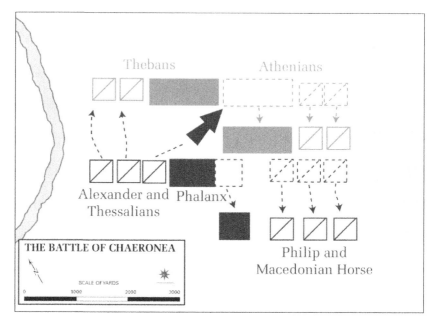

Fig. 12. Courtesy of the Department of History, United States Military Academy.
(Infantry: solid rectangles; cavalry: hollow rectangles)

He was only twenty years old when his father, Philip II of Macedon, was killed. His lack of experience, however, did not prevent him from taking bold actions to hinder his enemies and build his power base. Alexander's rapid and decisive reactions helped him gain the approval of the Macedonian people, who followed very closely the challenges that he had to overcome. His generosity and respect toward his people and other nations was evident during the first years of his worldwide campaign. Unfortunately, as time passed and the world gradually submitted to him, his nobility started to decrease. The more he conquered, the less patient he became.

The king always honored his dead soldiers, buried them properly, and provided compensations for their relatives, like tax exceptions for life. Except for special cases, he allowed proper burial for enemy soldiers who fell in combat and showed respect to brave defeated opponents. He punished the betrayers of other nations' kings, as he did with Bessus, the murderer of Darius. He showed deep devotion to Greek gods and reverence for other nations' deities. All the foregoing, he knew, helped him gain the favor of soldiers and civilians from Macedonia, its allies, and the newly annexed territories.

He was mostly a fair ruler and protected unfortunate persons from unfair practices. Bactrians and Sogdians, for example, used to throw out their sick and elderly to be devoured by dogs. Alexander stopped this terrible practice.[3]

The Liberator Role

Alexander believed that those who live under the same king should have the same rights. His revolutionary ideas and his ability to persuade the masses made him dangerous for his enemies. His vision of a new world where each city would keep its culture, religion, currency, laws, and taxes, represented a change in how kings ruled their domains. He ended the oligarchic regimes established by the Persians and returned the cities to their original laws, substituting the Persian satraps for Greco-Macedonians or native ones. As in the traditional Greek system, the building blocks of this new empire were the cities, with increased democratic and administrative autonomy. Having their own laws and customs restored, those cities no longer lived by the rules of a foreign and distant king.

Unlike previous Greek rulers, he did not want to punish cities but, rather, he wanted to create a gigantic state with a centralized administrative system with himself as the sovereign of this new empire. Alexander believed that treating people with contempt, particularly enemies, would only strengthen them.

"My rule is not tyrannical even in the case of conquered peoples," he said. "I did not come into Asia to wipe out its races entirely or to transform half of the world into a desert."[1] At Babylon, he ordered the restoration of the temple of Bel—god of the earth venerated by Babylonians—and of other temples destroyed by the Great King of Persia Xerxes I.

As time passed, however, Alexander slowly abandoned the role of liberator and became more a conqueror. The more he advanced, the farther he wanted to go—and nothing stopped him. Either by persuasion or by force, every city and nation was gradually falling under his power.

Respect for the Defeated

"Nothing is harder to direct than a man in prosperity; nothing more easily managed than one in adversity," said the Greek biographer Plutarch.⁵ Alexander often remarked that he did not want the people he conquered to regret his victory. "You have men fighting along with you and shedding blood for your empire," he said to his people, "who would have rebelled had they been treated disdainfully. Possession achieved by the sword is not of long duration, but gratitude for kindness shown is everlasting. If we wish to hold Asia and not merely pass through it we must impart our clemency to these people—it is their loyalty which will make our empire stable and enduring."⁶

Alexander showed uncommon respect to the relatives of his defeated enemies, especially to female nobility, even during times of war. After the Battle of Issus, Darius' wife, mother, and children became Macedonian hostages when the Persians fled the battlefield. The first thing Alexander did when he found out about his new captives was to inform them that Darius was alive, since Alexander knew that they were worried about Darius' life. Alexander even wept, seeing the devotion of Darius' family to the Persian king.

Those hostages could have been valuable for political negotiation. Alexander, however, never used them for this purpose. On the contrary, he granted them royal status, for example, giving the rank of queen to Darius' mother, because Darius was the one he was fighting, not his family. Alexander gave them dresses and jewelry and let them dwell undisturbed in their own accommodations. The Persian queen, whom Alexander called *my lady* and *your majesty*, and even Darius himself, thanked Alexander for his kindness and respect toward the captives. The Macedonian did not take advantage of his prisoners to increase his political power by forcing a marriage with Darius' daughter either. Only after nine years, and after Darius had died, did Alexander marry her.

Darius' servants had informed him about the treatment that Alexander gave to his family. So amazed was the Persian that he said to the gods, "Before all else make firm my rule; but my next prayer, if my career is at an end, is that Asia find no other ruler than this just enemy, this merciful victor."[7] Alexander, however, made it clear that he did not intend to make friends with Darius. He did not fight prisoners and women; his opponent must be armed.

After capturing Babylon and Susa by November 331 B.C., Alexander sat on the royal throne of Darius. Alexander was shorter than the Persian king was, and therefore his feet did not reach the step at the bottom. Noticing this, one of the royal pages placed a table under the Macedonian's feet. Perceiving some suffering on the part of a eunuch who had previously served Darius, Alexander asked him what was troubling him. The eunuch answered that Darius used to eat at that table, and he could not avoid weeping seeing the discourteous new use of the sacred table. Alexander felt shame for his unintentional offense and ordered the table removed, but Philotas asked him not to do so. "Take this as an omen, too," said Philotas, "the table from which your foe ate his banquets has been made a stool for your feet."[8]

After being betrayed and wounded by Bessus' friends in July 330 B.C., Darius recognized Alexander's kindness to his mother, wife, and children for the last time. He asked the gods to reward

Alexander for his humanity toward him and grabbing the hand of the loyal Polystratus, told him to give Alexander his right hand. When Alexander arrived, Darius was already dead. The Macedon showed deep sorrow and, stripping his own cloak off, covered Darius' body with it.

Alexander sent Darius' body to the Persian's mother so she could give her son a proper royal burial at Persepolis as other Persian kings had received. Darius' children received from Alexander the education and upbringing they would have received if Darius had remained a king. In addition, Alexander allowed Darius' brother to retain his royal status and even admitted him into the Macedon king's circle of friends.

Alexander showed a particular respect for women, especially for those of royal lineage. On one occasion, some female captives were singing at a banquet, and the king noticed that one of them was particularly shy and low in spirit. Her beauty was remarkable, and her humility attractive. Alexander suspected that she was royalty and asked her who she was. She was the granddaughter of the previous Persian king Ochus and the ex-wife of Hystaspes, a former commander and relative of Darius. Alexander was touched to learn how such unfortunate events had changed her life completely, so he ordered her release and the return of all her possessions to her. He further ordered his men to search for her husband, wherever he was, so they could be reunited.

The young king showed respect for the defeated on numerous occasions, but that quality was more evident during his first years as a king. Yet, his kindness did not disappear completely as he gained unmatched power.

After defeating King Porus in an extraordinary battle in the year 326 B.C., Alexander met face to face with this brave king who had fought admirably for his country. "What do you wish that I should do with you?" asked the Macedonian. "Treat me as a king ought,"[9] replied Porus. Alexander accepted the request and asked Porus if he wanted something for himself, but Porus replied that all he wanted appeared in his petition. Porus' nobility impressed Alexander deeply, so he reinstated Porus as king and even added other territories to his command. From that time on, Alexander had in Porus a faithful and courageous friend.

Cross-Cultural Leadership

Alexander had a global goal, but he acted locally to accomplish it. He was extremely sensitive to cultural differences among nations and realized that varied cultures required different styles of leadership. He customized his leadership style according to the values and the cultures of each nation. For instance, he used different arguments to get the support of Greek cities than those he used to get the approval of the annexed Persian territories.

Alexander used different characteristics for different nations. He knew that Greeks appreciated his education and culture, acquired from Aristotle, as well as his devotion to Greek gods. Macedonians loved his courage and his bold aspirations and the fact that he was Macedonian too. Egyptians respected the omens that proclaimed him a son of Zeus and his impressive record of achievements. Persians admired his cosmopolitan ideals and the opportunity to be treated as victors, even though they had been defeated in the battlefields.

Alexander promoted intermarriage between different cultures, especially between Persians and Macedonians, believing that this would help to consolidate his empire. He wanted the conquerors to shake off their arrogance and the defeated to get rid of their shame. Alexander himself, as the mythical Achilles had done before, married foreign and captive women. He married Roxane first, a barbarian of notable beauty, daughter of Oxyartes of Bactria, and afterward he married Barsine, also known as Stateira, the first-born daughter of Darius. According to the historian Aristobulus, Alexander also married Parysatis, the youngest daughter of Ochus, hence relating himself to both sides of the Persian royal family. As the king married wives from conquered nations, foreign people felt affection for him. His image gradually changed from a foreign conqueror and enemy to a just king whom they started to love.

He encouraged Macedonians and Greeks to learn things from natives. He did this, in part, because he knew that integration would be helpful to rule his growing diverse empire, but also because he acknowledged that his people could benefit from foreign ideas, military equipment, and soldiers. He adopted Persian dress, dipped his wine from the same bowl that foreigners did, and honored foreign deities—among other gestures—to unite the people of his empire and to govern them in harmony.

The Macedonian king wanted to eliminate the distinction between the conquered and the conquerors. To become the king of Europe, Africa, and Asia, he had to make sure that all continents benefited from the same privileges, so conquered nations would not feel that their new king was a complete foreigner. He included foreign soldiers in the Macedonian units, gave them Macedonian arms, and made them permanent members of his army. Furthermore, he regarded foreign military as fellow citizens and soldiers with family ties, rather than drafted troops. Alexander sought diversity within his team.

Some Macedonians and Greeks, however, did not like Alexander's ideas of integration, in particular the Persian marriage ceremonies and his new clothes. Those Macedonians and Greeks became jealous, noticing that Alexander's dependence on his fellow compatriots was diminishing. He was receptive to their concerns, but he did not change his ideas of integration between the conquered and the conquerors.

Chapter IX

Superior Team

"No man will make a great leader who wants to do it all himself or get all the credit for doing it." [1] *Andrew Carnegie*

N O ONE FIGHTS alone. Success is usually the result of a good team effort. Organizations usually acknowledge the significance of the team, but they sometimes overlook the importance of the *appropriate* team.

Selecting the Appropriate People

"In the end," said Warren Buffett, "we must have people to match our principles, not the reverse." [2] Alexander selected his soldiers very carefully, in particular the Companions, those who fought around him and helped him make crucial decisions. After all, Alexander would trust them not only with the destiny of Macedonia, but also with his dream and with his own life. They guarded the destiny of Macedonia until he died, helped him to achieve his outrageous dream, and saved his life several times.

Jim Collins, author of *Good to Great*, stated that the executives who transformed companies from good to great said, in essence, "Look, I don't really know where we should take this bus. But I know this much: If we get the right people on the bus, the right people in the right seats, and the wrong people off the bus, then we'll figure out how to take it someplace great."[3] Collins did an excellent job of highlighting and supporting the importance of getting and keeping the *right* people on the bus. Additionally, he found evidence that "It is who you pay, not how you pay them,"[4] what really matters in taking a company from good to great.

Empowering the Team

After selecting the appropriate people for each job, Alexander did what every good leader needs to do. He empowered his people so they could develop their full potential and transform goals into reality. Had Alexander been a micromanager, he could not have continued to advance toward the limits of the unknown, for he would have been too busy dealing with the affairs of the nations he had already conquered. He needed to delegate in order to let his empire grow, even if the risk seemed big.

Only God can be everywhere, and even though some people compared Alexander with a deity, he needed to delegate power to loyal first-class soldiers to manage the various affairs of his vast and ever-growing empire.

"Don't tell people how to do things," said George S. Patton, "tell them what to do and let them surprise you with their results."[5] Alexander empowered his people to govern annexed territories as well as to lead units of the Macedonian army. Generally, he would tell his commanders what they needed to achieve rather than how to do it, and he would only get involved if the situation turned worrisome. Though he knew his commanders could eventually make mistakes, the king encouraged judicious risk-taking.

Frequently, Alexander assigned important parts of his army to different outstanding leaders who served as his generals and sent them to separate routes or to distant nations with specific objectives. Those operations included, but were not limited to, pacifying revolts, negotiating with locals, annexing new territories, inspecting terrains, performing strategic maneuvers, diverting enemies' attention, and providing support and preemptive defense to the advances of the main force. Among some others, Nearchus, Ptolemy, the son of Lagus, Craterus, and Hephaestion headed these kinds of missions. While these commanders' expeditions were not unbeatable like Alexander's were, they were, for the most part, very successful and vital for the Macedonian king's plans.

Training and Preparation

"Private victories," says Stephen Covey in *The Seven Habits of Highly Effective People*, "precede public victories."[6] The Macedonians and their allies fought some of their battles seriously outnumbered by the enemy, and in most cases impeded by the difficulties of the terrain or fortifications. Furthermore, they had to fight all their battles in enemy terrain. To offset those major disadvantages, one of the various resources employed by Alexander was the intensive training of his troops. From the common soldiers to the highest commanders, Alexander's troops breathed combat and endurance; they were hungry for glory. From a young age, Macedonian soldiers were trained physically and physiologically for war and conquest.

Prepared for difficulties, they were very efficient in times of crisis and had an unusual ability to cope with hardships. Through continuous and seamless practice, their outstanding skills became second nature and did not fail them under extreme pressure. As Martina Navratilova said, "Every great shot you hit, you've already hit a bunch of times in practice."[7]

Albeit exaggerated, Alexander's assertion to his troops before the Battle of Issus was for the most part accurate. "They, no match for us either in bodily strength or resolution, will find their superiority in numbers of no avail. They," continued Alexander, "are Medes and Persians, men who for centuries have lived soft and luxurious lives; we of Macedon for generations past have been trained in the hazard school of danger and war."[8] In fact, the superior preparation of Alexander's troops helped counterbalance the overwhelming numerical superiority of the Persians. The Companions, one of the finest and best-trained cavalry units in history, charged relentlessly against the Persians and played a key role in the outcome of the battle.

Charidemus, an exiled Athenian who worked for Darius, had warned the Persian king about the Macedonians' outstanding preparation.

"The Macedonian line," explained Charidemus, "is certainly coarse and inelegant, but it protects behind its shields and lances immovable wedges of tough, densely-packed soldiers. The Macedonians call it a phalanx, an infantry column that holds its ground." He went on saying, "They wait eagerly for their commander's signal, and they are trained to follow the standards and not break ranks. To a man they obey their orders. Standing ground, encircling maneuvers, running to the wings, changing formation—the common soldier is no less skilled at all this than the officer. And don't think that what motivates them is the desire for gold and silver; until now such strict discipline has been due to poverty's schooling. When they are tired, the earth is their bed; they are satisfied with food they can prepare while they work; their sleeping time is of shorter duration than the darkness."[9]

Ironically, the previous warning, followed by a critique to the Persian army, cost Charidemus his life, for Darius took his words as an offense. Even before being executed, Charidemus kept telling Darius that he would pay the price for rejecting his warnings.

Charidemus was right about the spirit and training of Macedonians. Alexander made sure that his troops did not lose their spirit and turn lazy when they had time to relax. He organized contests based on military bravery, among other activities, assigning judges and giving rewards to the winners.

The Whole Greater than the Sum of its Parts

Alexander was an excellent individual performer, yet he had the wisdom to think interdependently and act as a team player. The coordination, mutual encouragement, and support within Alexander's team improved the synergy of the group, making the combined force a multiple, rather than a sum, of its participants.

The Battle of Gaugamela, like many others in Alexander's campaigns, demonstrated the ability of an interdependent small team to beat a gigantic opponent. Alexander told his officers of the necessity to comply with instructions quickly and transmit them to their respective units. All soldiers were to remember that the fortune of the entire army depended on the performance of each one of them. If every soldier performed his job properly, the victory, according to Alexander, was guaranteed; on the other hand, if one of them failed in his task, the entire military force would be in danger. During the battle, the diverse units of Alexander's army combined and coordinated their efforts in such a cohesive way that the Persians could not break them.

Although the Macedonians and their allies were at risk during the entire battle (Perdicas, Coenus, and Menidas were almost killed by arrows, while Hephaestion was wounded in the arm), their team performance and timing were exquisite. The Agrarian cavalry, for example, was fast enough to attack and force into retreat those Persians who were surrounding Alexander, when the king was assaulting the Persian front line. Later, Alexander's victory against Darius helped Parmenio to survive and to have his opportunity to succeed against a superior division led by Mazaeus.

As in any other successful team, rivalries and occasional disagreements among some members took place. Those differences, however, vanished during critical moments, and all members gave each other unconditional help, knowing that their final destiny—and survival—depended on the performance of the entire group. Additionally, Alexander was explicitly against internal fights and disputes, reacting fast and firmly as soon as he noticed them.

On one occasion, Hephaestion and Craterus, who had argued before, drew on each other, cheered on by their respective friends. Hephaestion liked to emulate the king's new habits of integration with annexed nations. He was a close friend of Alexander *the man,* and Alexander showed great affection for him. Craterus, on the other hand, was a close friend of Alexander *the king,* and Alexander had great respect for him. Craterus, unlike Hephaestion, was conservative about the customs and manners of Macedonia.

When Alexander heard about the fight, he rebuked both of them harshly. Afterward, he called both Hephaestion and Craterus to meet him, and he reconciled them. He said that he loved the two of them, but that if he ever saw them arguing again he would kill the provoker or both of them. After that episode, Hephaestion and Craterus never offended each other again.

Trusting the Right People

In a joint study conducted by the UCLA Graduate School of Management and Korn/Ferry International of New York City, 71 percent of the 1,300 senior executives surveyed declared that integrity is the quality most needed to succeed in business.[10] "In looking for people to hire," says Warren Buffett, "you look for three qualities: integrity, intelligence, and energy. And if they don't have the first, the other two will kill you."[11] All the good qualities of a follower will turn against the leader if the follower lacks integrity. Ironically, the greater the qualities of an unethical follower, the riskier he or she becomes for the leader and the organization. A good leader must not empower someone he or she distrusts.

For the most part, Alexander had a very good eye in choosing loyal leaders from different parts of the world. Nevertheless, foreign rulers whom he barely knew occasionally betrayed him. Plots against his life were made, particularly after he became extremely powerful. In those times, it was common to attempt to kill a king, and more kings were murdered by their own subjects than by their enemies. The participation of an officer close to Alexander in a conspiracy, however, was rarely if ever confirmed. For those who deceived him, death was the kindest punishment they received. Alexander considered loyalty a two-way street, and he was ruthless with those who betrayed his confidence. Of all the leaders in ancient history, he was the one you would not want to betray.

To minimize the risk of encouraging a possible traitor, Alexander decided to divide the control of certain nations and units to avoid concentration of power. The potential power of Egypt, for instance, did not escape Alexander's attention. He did not want to leave the entire control of that powerful country in the hands of one person only, so he split the authority among several officers. Many years later, the Romans remembered Alexander's lesson and split the authority in Egypt as well. On another occasion, the king split the cavalry into two different parts to divide control over that vital force.

The loyalty of Alexander's officers became more evident and stronger during critical moments. Those specially selected men who fought around him did not desire to outlive their king and showed little regard for their own lives when he was in danger. Alexander owed his life to the courage of those faithful officers. Cleitus saved his life at Granicus by cutting Rhoesaces' arm just before the Persian could strike at Alexander from behind. Peucestas, Abreas, and Leonnatus protected the Macedonian king with their own bodies during the campaign against the Mallians.

While Alexander was in Bactria, Erigyius and his Macedonian army were in Arian territory fighting against the deserter satrap of Aria, Satibarzanes. Noticing that the battle was flagging, Satibarzanes moved to the front line; and taking off his helmet, he challenged to a duel anyone who was willing to contest him. Erigyius was already an old soldier, but he could not stand Satibarzanes' arrogance; he removed his helmet and, showing his silver hair, said: "The day has arrived on which I shall show by victory or by an honourable death the quality of Alexander's friends and fighting men."[12]

Then he advanced toward his young enemy while the soldiers from both sides made an open space for the duel. Satibarzanes threw his lance first, and Erigyius avoided it with a small head movement. Then the Macedonian pressed forward with his horse and pierced his enemy's throat with a spear. Satibarzanes still fought back after he was wounded, but Erigyius removed the spear from his neck and struck it again in his face. After Satibarzanes' death, his soldiers, who had followed him under pressure, joined Erigyius' troops—and therefore Alexander's. Shortly after this episode, Erigyius met Alexander, who was chasing Bessus, and showed his king a war trophy—Satibarzanes' head.

Alexander was noticeably good at choosing generals and appointing new governors. He admired courageous and talented leaders, and he genuinely recognized those traits, even in his enemies. After defeating King Porus and the Indians in a remarkable battle during 326 B.C., Alexander met personally with the brave king who had fought commendably for his nation and had kept fighting even after the battle was completely lost.

Alexander was deeply impressed by Porus' courage and dignity. The Macedonian respected and trusted Porus' personality, and so he reinstated Porus as king, even adding territories to his command. As a result, Alexander gained a loyal and courageous friend who would help him with his campaign in India.

The Macedonian's good eye for trustworthy people went beyond hiring good soldiers. Once when he was sick—because of exhaustion or bathing in the extremely cold waters of the Cydnus River—most of his doctors were afraid to medicate him for fear of being accused of his murder. One of his trusted physicians, Philip the Acarnanian, proposed a medication to which Alexander agreed. Meanwhile, Parmenio had sent a letter to his king saying he had been informed that Darius had bribed Philip to poison Alexander.

Such was Alexander's confidence in Philip that he handed the note to him and drank the medicine while the doctor was still reading it. Philip explained that nothing was wrong with the medicine and told Alexander to follow his directions. Alexander did so, and in time recovered from his serious illness.

Chapter X

Superb Strategy

"The challenge of developing or reestablishing a clear strategy is often primarily an organizational one and depends on leadership."

Michael Porter[1]

LEADERSHIP AND STRATEGY cannot be separated. Professor Willie Pietersen (Columbia Business School) explains that no leader can lead effectively without a clear and compelling strategy to provide direction. Nevertheless, a strategy, no matter how brilliant it is, is going to take you nowhere without effective leadership because you have to win the hearts and minds of everybody behind the strategy if you're going to make it operational.[2]

But what is strategy? *Merriam-Webster Dictionary* defines strategy as the art of devising or employing plans or stratagems toward a goal.[3] Strategy, however, should not be confused with planning.

Strategies are plans, but not every plan is a strategy—in fact, very few are.

Bruce Greenwald, professor at Columbia Business School, and Judd Kahn, investment manager, say that strategies are indeed plans for achieving and sustaining success. But they are not just any ideas. Strategies are those plans that specifically focus on the actions and responses of competitors. Another important distinction made by Greenwald and Kahn, also emphasized by chess players, is the difference between strategy and tactic. In their view, strategic decisions are those whose results depend on the actions and reactions of other economic entities. In contrast, tactical decisions are ones that can be made in isolation and hinge largely on effective implementation.[4,5]

Alexander liked to develop his strategic plans by thinking of his own moves and his opponents' countermoves as if they were a chess game. After each real move, he would reassess the new position, looking for new alternatives to break his opponent's defense and to strengthen his own. Simulating actions, finding or creating a weak link, and attacking by several means simultaneously, were some of the many strategies available in Alexander's arsenal.

Simulated Actions

In chess, the threat of an action is often more valuable than the action itself, because the opponent needs to allocate resources to defend against a menace that may never materialize. As a result, the threat immobilizes resources of the defender and creates a stressful situation in a certain part of the board, thus allowing the menacing party to surprise his or her enemy by conducting a real attack in a different place, manner, or time, or a combination of the foregoing.

Around 327/326 B.C. Alexander arrived at the city of Massaga. Upon his approach to the city walls, the defenders sent their mercenary troops to fight the Macedonians. Alexander realized that combat near the walls would not be beneficial for him because if he defeated the Indian mercenaries, as he was sure to do, they would be able to retreat and find protection inside the city.

He decided to drag the defenders away from the city so it would be more difficult for them to retreat. To achieve that, he ordered his troops to move back about a mile as soon as the mercenaries advanced toward them. This seeming indication of victory motivated the defenders to charge in a disorderly fashion away from the walls.

Following his initial strategy, Alexander sent the powerful phalanx, the cavalry, the archers, and the Agrianes against the Indians, while he led the infantry's advance in person. This unexpected and nicely coordinated attack caused serious losses among the defenders. Now escape was a hard task, and many defenders died before finding protection inside the city. The next day, Alexander brought the siege engines, and after four days of siege, the defenders capitulated.

Alexander used a similar strategy in 325 B.C. to defeat the rebel town of Harmatelia, in the territory of King Sambus. Sambus had agreed to surrender the towns of his kingdom to Alexander, but the people of Harmatelia refused to obey their king.

Alexander sent a small contingent toward the wall of the city, with instructions to incite the defenders, pretend a setback, and retreat gradually. When the Harmatelians pursued the *defeated* enemies, he attacked them at once with a lager unit that had remained hidden until that moment. The defenders opposed the Macedonians with poisoned swords, inflicting deadly wounds upon them. Nevertheless, the Macedonians killed about 600 natives and captured another 1,000, and the city of Harmatelia eventually capitulated.

By the year 326 B.C., Alexander was about to fight one of the last remarkable battles of his short life. He had previously subjugated by intimidation some Indian territories, and he expected to do the same with Porus, the king of the Pauravas. Porus, however, was determined to defend his territory and placed a massive army at the point of entry of his kingdom, on the far side of the river Hydaspes, to prevent the Macedonians from crossing. His army consisted of eighty-five gigantic elephants in the front line, 300 chariots and about 30,000 foot soldiers.

When the Macedonians arrived at the Hydaspes and saw the size of the river they had to cross, in addition to the enormous beasts awaiting for them on the far shore, they panicked. The Hydaspes did not offer any shallow place to be crossed in the summer. Alexander realized that attempting a crossing would have been suicidal because when his floating devices transporting the cavalry reached the opposite shore, the huge elephants and the horrendous Indian trumpeting would terrify his horses. Therefore, Alexander decided to force an opportunity to cross by simulated actions. Otherwise, he would wait for winter when the water would be low and crossing the river would be easier.

Alexander kept his enemy on guard by sending units to different points along the shore. This forced Porus and his people to be in constant movement, expecting Alexander's forces to cross the river. Porus split the Indian army and sent them in groups to several places to prevent Alexander's crossing. Every night Alexander would send the cavalry out at regular intervals to make battle sounds at different points along the shoreline. Porus himself followed those noises, moving his troops on the opposite side of the shore to prevent the Macedonians from crossing the river unexpectedly. These false alarms gave the Indians no time to relax or prepare for an organized defense at one place. After several days, Porus, tired of the game, stopped following those shouts and threats of an attack that never materialized, providing exactly the opportunity Alexander was seeking to create to catch Porus off guard.

Alexander decided to cross the river by concealing a crossing behind a wooded deserted island, which was about eighteen miles away from his original location and out of Porus' view. He resolved to lead the crossing himself, leaving Craterus in charge of the main camp and instructed him to initiate a crossing only if Porus decided to move toward Alexander's new position. Furthermore, Alexander instructed Craterus not to attack if Porus left the elephants on that part of the shore, since Alexander believed that those animals were the main threat to the cavalry.

To conceal his movements, Alexander asked Attalus, who looked similar to him from a distance, to dress in royal clothes, pretend to be the king, and stay with Craterus. Meanwhile, Alexander advanced, away from the shore so Porus could not see him, toward the deserted island. In between the island and Craterus' position, Alexander placed the mercenary cavalry and infantry with instructions to attack only after the Indians were occupied fighting him.

Under cover of night and a lucky rainfall, Alexander and his troops prepared for the crossing, which would use rafts and boats that had already been taken to that place. Before sunrise, the rain, which had helped to conceal the noises, stopped. The Macedonians were undertaking the first part of the crossing shielded by the island, so Porus' lookouts were still unaware of the danger. After passing the island, the Macedonians were easily spotted by the Indian scouts, who rushed to inform Porus about the imminent attack. Alexander disembarked unintentionally on a second island, believing it was the mainland, before he finally led the landing on the slippery shore. The strategy for making the crossing had worked perfectly.

Next, Alexander ordered his troops to form ranks and advance in battle order, with him at the head of his army toward Porus' position. Porus had sent his son to oppose the landing, but because of Alexander's speed, Porus' son could not prevent the crossing. When Alexander saw that Porus did not lead the Indian forces, he attacked immediately. The overnight rain had created mud, and the Indian chariots were bogged down. The Indian troops could not resist the attack and, seeing Alexander in person with his cavalry, they fled toward Porus' position. Many Indians, including Porus' son, were killed in this engagement.

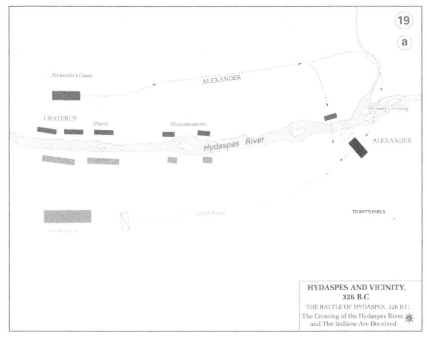

Fig. 13. Courtesy of the Department of History, United States Military Academy.
(Infantry: solid rectangles; cavalry: hollow rectangles)

Now, Porus had to decide whether to move toward Alexander, which would clear the way for Craterus to cross the river, or to wait for Alexander at his original location. He moved toward Alexander's position, but he left a small unit with elephants to prevent Craterus from crossing. Porus took a force of approximately

30,000 men, 200 elephants, 300 chariots, and 4,000 cavalry. He advanced until he found firm land, and there he stopped and prepared for battle. He placed the terrifying elephants in the front line, at intervals of about 100 feet. In the second line, filling the gaps between the elephants, he placed the infantry, which extended to both wings beyond the elephants. Last, Porus located the cavalry and the chariots at the end of both flanks to prevent an encircling maneuver.

Alexander did not rush to attack Porus, but he rather gained time to allow his troops to rest after the crossing of the river and the battle against Porus' son. In order to keep Porus guessing, Alexander ordered equestrian operations while the remaining forces recovered their strength. Soon, he started making the real disposition to fight Porus.

Alexander planned to personally lead a cavalry assault on Porus' left wing and send Coenus' unit to Porus' right with instructions to wait for the right moment to attack. That right moment would be when the Indians moved their equestrians to counter Alexander's assault on their left flank. Then Coenus would take advantage of the confusion to attack the enemy rear.

Alexander's strategy worked perfectly, and the battle started exactly as he had planned it. When Coenus was about to attack the Indians' rear, they were forced to split their forces, and Alexander launched his attack against the disordered Indian troops at that precise moment. Thanks to his strategy, the Macedonians destroyed their enemy's plan and won part of the battle before they even started to fight hand to hand.

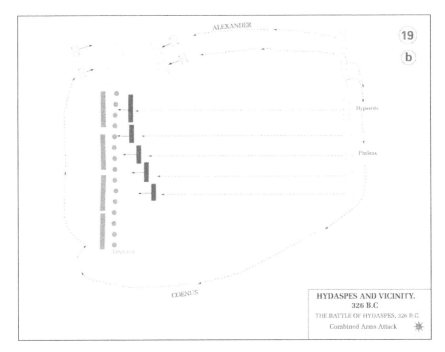

Fig. 14. Courtesy of the Department of History, United States Military Academy.
(Infantry: solid rectangles; cavalry: hollow rectangles)

Porus sent the elephants against the Macedonian cavalry, but with the infantry's help, the cavalry managed to resist the attack. The Macedonians charged against the Indian elephants and their riders, until the elephants, wounded and tired, began to retreat. Alexander had been waiting for that opportunity. He sent the compact phalanx formation to press against elephants and horses, inflicting numerous casualties and defeating the Indians. Porus had lost three sons, 20,000 foot soldiers, 3,000 equestrians, and many elephants, but he still kept fighting until Alexander, impressed by Porus' courage, rushed to save his enemy's life.

Out-of-the-Box Strategies

The capacity to come up with innovative and unconventional ideas has been a hallmark of many notable leaders and has set them apart from their contemporaries. Innovative leaders seem always to have an ace in the hole; they find alternatives and ingenious solutions to problems that represent a deadlock for others. Founders and champions of once unthinkable endeavors, like Larry Ellison and Bill Gates, tend to posses this valuable attribute. For example, ignoring conventional wisdom was a key success factor in Larry Ellison and Oracle's success.

Typically, a diverse education and broad experiences prepare leaders for out-of-the-box thinking and paradigm shifts. In the case of Alexander, poetry and music, more than warfare, had captured his attention during his childhood. When Alexander became a young man, Aristotle, one of the cleverest thinkers of ancient history, fed his hungry mind with a broad education that included philosophy, medicine, astronomy, geometry, political science, zoology, embryology, music, and poetry. Timotheus first and Homer afterward became Alexander's favorite poets.

As a conqueror and strategist, Alexander introduced several functional innovations. Among other things, he improved the original Syracusan catapult, doubling its range and improving its accuracy. His large siege engines spurred an evolution that led to impressive machines. He eliminated the former division of nationalities within the cavalries, implementing a more cohesive organization and basing the leadership of these units on merit, rather than race. Alexander created novelty units by blending Persian bowmen and slingers with his other soldiers. He also introduced new and more efficient methods to organize and signal the troops.

When Alexander dealt with the siege of the coastal city of Miletus, during 334 B.C., the Persian fleet seriously outnumbered him. Knowing that naval battles were not his strength, he developed an alternative strategy designed to avoid a naval confrontation and to win the sea battle from the ground. He located his ships at Miletus' harbor, placing them in the narrowest part of the entrance, very close to one another, so the port remained closed to the Persian fleet and the city became isolated.

By 330/329 B.C., Alexander was chasing Bessus and Satibarzanes through Arian territory. The Arians had taken advantage of the landscape, a rocky projection full of trees, to form a barricade and prevent the Macedonian advance. They had placed men on the only available pathway, chopped down numerous trees, and formed piles of trunks and stones. Advancing became almost impossible for the Macedonians, and going back was not an easy task either because of the nature of the terrain.

Alexander evaluated his options, but none of them seemed good enough to overcome the obstacles; after reconsidering several alternatives, he created an unconventional strategy. He noticed that the wind was blowing toward his enemies, so he ordered his men to cut down trees, to gather them, and to set fire to them. After his soldiers had piled up a considerable number of trees and lit a fire, the wind did the rest of the work by blowing the flames toward his enemies. Soon, the fire started to kill the Arians, and Alexander redeployed his people so that those Arians who could escape the fire, either died in the hands of the Macedonians or killed themselves by jumping from the cliffs.

Anticipating Opponents' Moves

"Chance," said Louis Pasteur, "favors only the prepared mind."[6] The best chess players spend significant time thinking of their opponent's future moves. For each one of their own moves, they need also to anticipate how their adversary will respond. No matter how good a player may be at planning his or her own moves, the player's strategy will fail if he or she does not accurately anticipate the antagonist's reactions. Chess players know that after each one of their moves, it is their opponents' turn to play. In real life, we sometimes forget that our opponents have the right to play too, and that they will exercise that right. Underestimating the intelligence of one's opponent could be suicidal.

"The good fighters of old," wrote Sun Tzu before Alexander was born, in his book *The Art of War*, "first put themselves beyond the possibility of defeat, and then waited for an opportunity of defeating the enemy."[7] Before every battle, Alexander would spend time anticipating his enemies' possible responses and developing strategies to prevent them. At Gaugamela (October 331 B.C.), he predicted that Darius would take advantage of his vast army and would attempt a flank attack, or even worst, an encircling maneuver. To prevent this chance, Alexander kept his line advancing at an angle, still presenting a solid front line. This strategy had a dual purpose: first, to make it difficult for the Persians to encircle his army, and second, to meet face to face with Darius, who was commanding one of the wings. Alexander had applied a similar precautionary maneuver when he crossed the Granicus River (April-June 334 B.C.) into Asia Minor. To avoid a flank attack when his troops were coming out of the water, Alexander added combined cavalry and foot units at the angle of each wing, hiding his soldiers among the equestrians.

The first of Darius' attacks during the Battle of Gaugamela, which Alexander anticipated masterfully also, was the advance of the Persian scythe chariots. The Persians possessed numerous war chariots which the Macedonians lacked, and the Persians planned to send them against Alexander's first line to break his formation, cause confusion, and kill numerous soldiers. Alexander predicted this attack and instructed his archers and javelin throwers to start shooting at the chariot drivers as soon as they were within missile range. This action would minimize the impact of the Persian offensive. Then, his front line would intentionally break its formation and let the scythe chariots pass; the Royal Guard would be waiting for those chariots behind the Macedonian front.

As planned, the chariots were allowed to break into the Macedonian ranks and soon faced the compact phalanx.

The Macedonians stabbed the horses, surrounded the chariots, and killed the charioteers. Even though the Persians' chariots killed a few Macedonians, Alexander's strategy worked smoothly and averted an early strike that could have changed the outcome of the battle. This strategy of Alexander was later remembered by Napoleon, who then added that the whole art of war consists of a well-reasoned and circumspect defensive followed by a rapid and audacious attack.[8]

Alexander's ability to anticipate dangers was not restricted to battlefield tactics. He planned his future major strategic moves beforehand, paying special attention to what his enemies could be doing in the meantime.

When Alexander learned that Tyrians wanted to keep their neutrality (332 B.C.), he called for a meeting of the Companions and other officers to analyze the details of this new situation. "I do not see how we can safely advance upon Egypt," he said, "so long as Persia controls the sea; and to pursue Darius with the neutral city of Tyre in our rear and Egypt and Cyprus still in enemy hands would be a serious risk, especially in view of the situation in Greece. With our army on the track of Darius, far inland in the direction of Babylon, the Persians might well regain control of the coast, and thus be enabled with more power behind them to transfer the war to Greece, where Sparta is already openly hostile to us, and Athens, at the moment, is but an unwilling ally; fear, not friendliness, keeping her on our side. But with Tyre destroyed, all Phoenicia would be ours."[9]

"The next step," continued Alexander, "will be Cyprus: it will either join us without trouble on our part, or be easily taken by assault; then, with the accession of Cyprus and the united fleets of Macedon and Phoenicia, our supremacy at sea would be guaranteed, and the expedition to Egypt would thus be a simple matter, and finally, with Egypt in our hand we shall have no further cause for uneasiness about Greece."[10]

This type of analysis was typical of Alexander, and was designed to anticipate how the international chessboard would look after his and his opponents' moves, both political and military. He had no difficulty in communicating his strategy and convincing his people. He carried on with the strategy systematically, and he finally departed from Egypt, venerated as a god, in the spring of 331 B.C.

Creating and Seizing Opportunities

Opportunities are difficult to find, and more difficult to recognize as such. A leader should be able to find, recognize, and capitalize on opportunities. A great leader also must create opportunities when they seem to be scarce or nonexistent. As Edward de Bono said, "Opportunity ideas do not lie around waiting to be discovered. Such ideas need to be produced."[11]

During the Battle of Gaugamela, after the Macedonians had stopped the advance of the scythe chariots, the Persian horsemen attempted to encircle the Macedonian right, by taking advantage of their much larger front line. Alexander responded to Darius' move by sending Aretes to reinforce the right side and to attack the enemy's cavalry. Further, Alexander noticed that the movement of the Persian cavalry had left a weak link in his enemy's front line. He rushed toward that gap with the Companions and the heavy infantry located in that area. By doing so, he placed the best people he had, including himself, so they could seize the biggest opportunity. "Effective executives," Peter Drucker said, "put their best people on opportunities rather than on problems." Later he added that problem solving, however necessary, does not produce results. It prevents damage. Exploiting opportunities produces results.[12]

Alexander led a furious attack against the Persians on that right zone, and the Persians could not resist for long the combined attack of the Companions and the phalanx. Having seized the opportunity to break the Persian front line, Alexander advanced to fight Darius at the head of his troops.

The battle of Alexander against King Porus showed three key moments where the Macedonian capitalized on his opportunities. The first opportunity, created by Alexander, was getting Porus tired and confused by menacing various attacks at different locations. The second opportunity was the island used by the Macedonians to hide from the Indians and cross the river. The third one was also created by Alexander by attacking the Indians' left wing and sending Coenus to their right. Alexander seized the three opportunities and attained a remarkable victory.

Another strategy utilized by Alexander to create opportunities was to attack his enemies by several means at once. He created confusion in his opponents' lines, forced a weak link, and exploited it.

Many business leaders have successfully used these strategies, and other strategies discussed in this book, in contemporary corporate settings. Alexander's strategies inspired leaders like Ted

Turner, founder of CNN, who said, "a new business venture is like a military campaign: You have to think it through; you have to work hard, figure things out very carefully; you've got to motivate employees, you've got to get everybody pumped up."[13]

Many other business leaders have applied Alexander's legendary concepts, perhaps without even knowing it. Larry Ellison, Michael Dell, and Bill Gates had to overcome paradigms and preconceived ideas as Alexander did through his campaigns to achieve remarkable business successes at Oracle, Dell, and Microsoft. Also like Alexander, Jack Welch, former CEO of General Electric, strived to anticipate his opponents' moves and adapted GE's strategy accordingly before it was too late. Global companies like Coca-Cola and McDonald have learned the lesson of integration—vital to lead in a multicultural business word. Warren Buffet shined in managing the reputation of Berkshire Hathaway, knowing that a mistaken perception could cost millions of dollars to his company and its constituencies. Goldman Sachs' leaders have mastered the concept of selecting the appropriate people and building a superior team, which gave the company an enviable position in the financial world. Steve Jobs has consistently come up with out-of-the-box strategies and innovations in order to position Apple as a leading edge company. The two iconic leaders of the Private Equity industry, archrivals Stephen Schwarzman and Henry Kravitz, have successfully used secrecy and surprise in most of the acquisitions they have made.

Chapter XI

The Element of Surprise

"The backbone of surprise is fusing speed with secrecy."[1]

Karl von Clausewitz

WHETHER IN POLITICS, warfare, business, or sport, being unpredictable to one's rival pays off. Almost every good leader recognizes the benefits of surprising one's opponent. The leader who surprises his adversary may find that adversary unprepared without the time to get organized, and he or she may react emotionally rather than rationally to the surprise.

The Prussian general and military strategist Karl von Clausewitz proposed a precise definition of surprise: "The backbone of surprise is fusing speed with secrecy." Alexander illustrated this at Issus.

Alexander and Darius did not meet at once in Issus, but rather they advanced during a few days trying to guess each other's position. Darius moved north, and when he learned that Alexander had just passed to the south, he advanced quickly to surprise him from the rear on the wide-open Assyrian Plains. With this movement, Darius also aimed to cut Alexander's access to supplies. Alexander, however, surprised the Persian king by changing course and meeting Darius at a much more advantageous place for the small Macedonian army: the narrower plain of Issus.

Right before the battle, Alexander continued to use surprise effectively. Darius recalled the cavalry he had previously sent across the river and redirected most of it to his right to pressure Parmenio's position on the seaside as the ground there was more favorable for his equestrians. Aware of the danger, Alexander sent the Thessalian equestrians to his left wing to support Parmenio. They executed the maneuver with speed and secrecy at the rear of the infantry to hide it from the Persian view.

Alexander noticed some weakness on his right wing and the possibility that the vast Persian army could outflank his troops. Hence, he relocated two squadrons of the Companions from the center to the right wing. Again, they rapidly executed the reposition maneuver behind the lines, fusing speed with secrecy. These two rapid actions gave the Macedonians a wider front than the Persians had, although Darius kept overwhelming reserve superiority behind the front line.

The battle finally started with another surprising action from the Macedonian ranks. Alexander, located at the right of his army, crossed a stream at full speed and led an unexpected cavalry attack. The strike shocked the Persian left, which broke down almost immediately, and minimized the damage inflicted by the Persian archers.

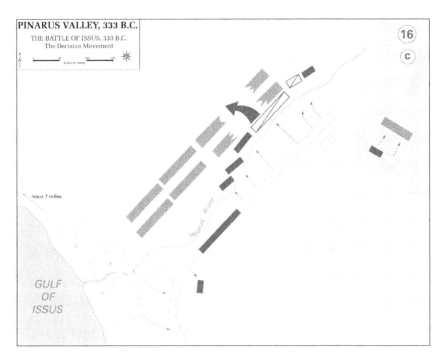

Fig. 15. Courtesy of the Department of History, United States Military Academy.
(Infantry: solid rectangles; cavalry: hollow rectangles)

A good part of surprise depends on timing. On most occasions, leaders need to wait for the right time before acting. Once the timing for the action has been determined, however, said action must be carried out with speed to maximize the surprise effect on the antagonist. That is precisely what Alexander did when he fought King Porus. He kept Porus guessing for a while, waiting for the right timing to attack him. When Porus least expected it, Alexander launched a secret and decisive attack.

Secrecy

Another important factor of surprise is to conceal the furtive act as much as possible, because the consequences of the surprise tend to be more powerful. To surprise his enemies Alexander often took the most difficult route—the one that no one, not even the locals, would expect him to choose.

That was the case during the campaign against the Uxians. By the end of 331 B.C., after defeating Darius for the second time in the Battle of Gaugamela and capturing Babylon, Alexander departed to the province of Persia, crossed the Pasitigris, and entered the land of the Uxians. The Uxians, who occupied the plains, were loyal to the Persian satrap and surrendered to Alexander without presenting resistance.

Those who lived in the hills, however, were not under Persian dominion and sent a message to Alexander indicating they would not allow him to cross to Persia unless they received the same payment that they used to receive from the Persians. Alexander sent the messengers back home with an invitation to meet him at the passage, where he said he would give them what they wanted. He headed secretly during the night through a difficult and unexpected road reaching the villages within one day and attacking them before they were awake. Then he hurried to the passage and sent Craterus to take control of the high ground where the

Uxians would escape in the event of a fight. Thanks to his fast and secret move, Alexander reached the passage before the Uxians, and from there he moved down to the attack. The natives, taken by total surprise, did not try to resist the attack. Instead, they ran away. Some of them were killed as they tried to escape while Craterus killed those who made it to the high ground.

After defeating the Uxians, Alexander went to the Persian Gates, where Ariobarzanes, satrap of the province, was blocking the pass with a large army. First, Alexander attacked the pass, but the rain of missiles thrown by his enemy forced him to retreat. Alexander then planned a surprise attack. He would advance through a narrow and tricky surrounding route under cover of night. Craterus and his contingent would remain behind, waiting for instructions to attack the pass once again.

Alexander took with him the best detachments he had for this type of operation, advanced during the entire night, and before sunrise he launched a surprise attack against an outstation first and Ariobarzanes' core location second. Craterus, alerted by the signal of the trumpets, started a simultaneous attack on the external defenses of the pass.

This combined attack was too much for Ariobarzanes' army. With Alexander on one end, Craterus on the other, and Ptolemy attacking the center, Ariobarzanes' soldiers had no place to escape. Ariobarzanes and a few equestrians fled to the hills, but the rest perished at the Macedonians' hands.

Chapter XII

Negotiation: When and How

"The best battle is the battle that is won without being fought."

Sun Tzu[1]

A S A RULE, Alexander was willing to negotiate and build strategic alliances whenever that was possible and convenient for him. He always kept in mind, however, his alternatives to negotiation.

Determining beforehand the alternatives to a negotiation helps to minimize bad decisions. Unfortunately, some negotiators get so involved in the conflict that they lose sight of the big picture. In their book *Getting To Yes: Negotiating Agreement Without Giving In*, Fisher, Ury, and Patton formally introduce the concept of BATNA (Best Alternative to a Negotiated Agreement). These authors, of the Harvard Negotiation Project, say that whether you should or should not agree on something in a negotiation depends entirely upon the attractiveness to you of the best available alternative.[2]

Sharing Sun Tzu's belief that the best battle is the battle that is won without being fought, Alexander preferred to receive a friendly surrender proposal from his opponents, rather than to spend significant time and resources fighting against each city and country. Yet he was firm in stating and defending the matters that he considered nonnegotiable. Typically, Alexander's negotiation terms were not flexible. He did not present proposals to start a bargaining process although he accepted some reasonable requests as alternative solutions. The way Alexander dealt early in his reign with the rebellious city of Thebes is a good example of his willingness to negotiate and his firmness in doing so. He made every effort to reach a negotiated agreement and to preserve the peace and union of Greece, but when his BATNA became the best option, Alexander did not hesitate to use it.

Alexander gained a reputation as a trustworthy individual, which helped him as a negotiator. In times when international courts did not exist, the reputation of a negotiator was crucial. Alexander demanded from others the same level of commitment that he gave to his agreements, and he had no mercy for those who did not live up to their promises. His response to a breach of contract by the city of Aspendus was a demand for money and hostages. He totally annihilated Thebes for its second breach.

Alexander was sensitive to cultural differences when negotiating with other countries. Being aware of cross-border differences represents an important advantage for good negotiators, as not every culture has the same negotiation style. John Graham, professor of marketing and international business at the University of California, Irvine, found that in American negotiations, higher profits are achieved by making opponents feel uncomfortable, while in Japanese negotiations, higher profits are associated with making opponents feel comfortable.[3] Similarly, Michael Morris and Paul Ingram, professors of management at Columbia Business School, found that while Americans typically maintain some separation between their personal and professional lives, Chinese tend to establish almost family-like bonds with their business associates. This is one reason that business relationships take longer to establish in China. "In China, if you're going to do business with someone you start by forging a personal, affective bond—you exchange gifts, you have a series of meals together, you may be invited to meet their family. The personal bond paves the way toward a working relationship."[4]

When dealing with the city of Tyre, Alexander tried first to negotiate its surrender, knowing that a siege—if possible at all—would be extensive and affect his plans. Since the result of the war between Alexander and Darius was still open-ended, Tyrians considered it wise to remain neutral. Therefore, Alexander decided to use his best alternative and convinced the Companions to capture the city.

The negotiations that Alexander did pursue, however, were with other neighbor cities. He used the propaganda of his victory at Issus against Darius to convince other cities to provide him with vessels. Alexander knew that those cities had previously supported Persia because they had no choice, but now that he had defeated Darius once, those cities could consider a strategic alliance with the Macedonians. Because of these negotiations, Alexander received reinforcements of vessels from Phoenicia, Rhodes, Soli, Mallus, Lycia, and Cyprus.

In other circumstances, Alexander judged that the offer received was better than his best alternative. That was the case with the town of Celaenae. By the year 334/333 B.C., Alexander advanced toward Celaenae, but when he entered the city he found it deserted because the defenders had sheltered themselves in a stronghold. Alexander sent a messenger to tell the Celaenaeans that if they did not surrender to him, they would be severely punished. The defenders proposed a sixty-day armistice, after which they would surrender if they did not receive reinforcements from Darius.

Alexander knew that capturing the stronghold, which was located in a very elevated place, would demand a long siege and many lives. Hence, he decided to accept the unusual proposal. He left a force of 1,500 soldiers to watch the bastion and headed to Gordium. After the agreed upon period, no reinforcements had arrived to Celaenae, and the city surrendered to him.

When to Play Hardball

As time passed and his power ballooned, Alexander became less patient and more inclined to use hardball negotiation techniques. As Lewicki, Saunders, and Minton discuss in their book *Essentials of Negotiation*, hardball tactics work better against adversaries who are not well prepared for negotiation, but they can backfire because many people are motivated to seek revenge.[5] Alexander was more likely to play hardball when his goals were at odds with those of his adversaries (distributive bargaining, according to Lewicki), and he was more flexible when his interests were not mutually exclusive with those of his opponent (integrative negotiation, Lewicki).

After the Battle of Issus in November 333 B.C., where Alexander defeated Darius for the first time, but the Persian king managed to escape, Darius sent a letter to negotiate with Alexander. In the letter, Darius asked Alexander to release his wife, mother, and children in exchange for a friendship between Darius and Alexander; Darius would become Alexander's ally. Alexander's response was harsh:

> *Your ancestors invaded Macedonia and Greece and caused havoc in our country, though we had done nothing to provoke them. As supreme commander of all Greece I invaded Asia because I wished to punish Persia for this act—an act which must be laid wholly to your charge. You sent aid to the people of Perinthus in their rebellion against my father; Ochus* sent an army into Thrace, which was a part of our dominions; my father was killed by assassins whom, as you openly boasted in your letters, you yourselves hired to commit the crime; having murdered Arses with Bagoas' help,*

---

*Also named Artaxerxes III, and sometimes called Artaxerxes Ochus. King of Persia (358–338 B.C.).

you unjustly and illegally seized the throne, thereby committing a crime against your country; you sent the Greeks false information about me in the hope of making them my enemies; you attempted to supply the Greeks with money—which only the Lacedaemonians were willing to accept, your agents corrupted my friends and tried to wreck the peace which I had established in Greece—then it was that I took the field against you; but it was you who began the quarrel. First I defeated in battle your general and satraps; now I have defeated you and the army you led.

Alexander ended the letter saying:

And in the future let any communication you wish to make with me be addressed to the King of all Asia. Do not write to me as to an equal. Everything you possess is now mine; so, if you should want anything, let me know in the proper terms, or I shall take steps to deal with you as a criminal. If, on the other hand, you wish to dispute your throne, stand and fight for it and do not run away. Wherever you may hide yourself, be sure I shall seek you out.[6]

A few months after this exchange of letters, in January-August 332 B.C., Alexander received emissaries from Darius. These emissaries offered 10,000 talents in exchange for Darius' wife, mother, and children, and proposed that Alexander keep all the land west of the Euphrates River. Alexander was supposed to seal this alliance by marrying Darius' daughter. General Parmenio advised Alexander to accept the offer and said that, if he were Alexander, he would be pleased to finish the war on those favorable terms. However, Alexander had a different plan. He had not left Macedonia to capture a considerable part of Darius' huge empire; he left Macedonia with a much more ambitious idea. "That," replied Alexander to Parmenio's comment, "is what I should do were I Parmenio; but since I am Alexander, I shall send Darius a different answer."[7]

Alexander wrote back saying that he had no need of Darius' money, nor would he accept part of a continent instead of the whole. All Asia and its riches were already Alexander's property, and if he wanted to marry Darius' daughter, he would do it without Darius' approval. If Darius wanted contemplation from him, he should come to Alexander and ask for it in person.

After receiving this reply from Alexander, Darius abandoned any idea of reaching an agreement with the Macedonian and started to prepare for war one more time.

In other cases, Alexander's hardball tactics had better results. Many cities surrendered to him when they realized that his terms were inflexible, and that he preferred to fight rather than to accept a sub-optimal agreement. Surrendering and joining Alexander, rather than opposing him, was preferable for his enemies, because his retaliation was ruthless.

Building Meaningful Strategic Alliances

"Understanding the nature of the interdependence of the parties," say Lewicki, Saunders, and Minton, "is critical to successful negotiation."[8] Alexander understood that the enemies of his enemies were potential allies of his. He also knew that, by sharing something, like goals, desire for revenge, lineage, or culture, would better position him to get the support of other nations. He tried to capitalize on similarities without compromising his goals.

Alexander started to build his power base almost from scratch, after his father died, departing from Macedonia in 336 B.C. with a small army of 30,000 infantry and 5,000 cavalry. First, he invoked the common lineage that bonded Macedonians with Thessalians to get their support, political and military. Then he advanced toward the Peloponnese where he called for a meeting of their cities. The twenty-year-old Macedonian asked them to confirm him as the leader of the Greek alliance, evoking a previous agreement that they had made with his father. Here again, he managed to get their support, except for the Spartans. Getting the support of the south of Greece, however, was more difficult. Athens and other cities became reluctant allies of his, and he eventually decided to destroy Thebes to show his teeth to those who believed him weak.

Alexander built valuable strategic alliances in Asia Minor as well. He received, for instance, the assistance of Ada, a royal who was seeking to regain the control of Caria that she had lost after her husband—and brother—Hidrieus died. Since his death, she had remained in control of only Alinda, a very well-defended town of Caria. Ada was very fond of Alexander, and she wanted to adopt him as her son, an offer that he did not refuse. After Alexander seized Caria and won the loyalty of the Carians, who supported Ada's claim, he appointed Ada as governor of the entire region.

Soon after, in Asia Minor, Alexander dealt with the Pisidian city of Termessus, which was located on high and steep ground and controlled a passage to Phrygia. He made an alliance with the people of a neighbor town, Selga, who had been longtime enemies of Termessus, despite being also of the Pisidian bloodline. From that time on, Alexander found in the people of Selga very trustworthy allies.

Making strategic alliances with the enemies of his enemies was a common practice of Alexander. The valuable cooperation he received from those allies included troops, supplies, and tactical information about his enemies and the terrain. At Aornos, for example, he allied with natives who guided him to an assailable path to the nearly impregnable Rock. This type of assistance was crucial, given the Macedonians' unfamiliarity with most of the countries they conquered. In India, Alexander made an alliance with King Omphis, who was at war with two other local kings, Abisares and Porus. Omphis provided Alexander with 56 elephants, 3,000 bulls, numerous sheep, and lots of grain.

Building meaningful strategic alliances provides important benefits to the leader. It strengthens his or her position, prevents adversaries from getting the support of allies, and makes it more appealing for neutral parties to join him or her.

Chapter XIII

Relentless Hard Work

"There is no substitute for hard work."[1]

Thomas A. Edison

GOOD LEADERS ARE usually persistent and hard workers. They are intellectually and physically strong, with enough stamina to deal with demanding situations, even when they are tired or having a bad day. The persistence of those leaders inspires their followers and builds trust.

Among other leaders, several presidents of the United States have praised the virtues of perseverance and hard work.

Calvin Coolidge said, "Nothing in this world can take the place of persistence. Talent will not; nothing is more common than unsuccessful men with talent. Genius will not; unrewarded genius is almost a proverb. Education will not; the world is full of educated derelicts. Persistence and determination alone are omnipotent."[2]

Thomas Jefferson said, "I find that the harder I work, the more luck I seem to have."[3]

Theodore Roosevelt said, "I am only an average man but, by George, I work harder at it than the average man."[4]

Finally, John Quincy Adams said, "Patience and perseverance have a magical effect before which difficulties disappear and obstacles vanish."[5]

In addition to other accomplishments, we remember Alexander for the extreme length and difficulty of his marches and his persistence in besieging impregnable cities like Tyre and Gaza. During his campaigns, he traveled about 22,000 miles by foot and horseback.[6] When chasing Darius and Bessus in 330 B.C., Alexander and his army traveled hundreds of miles under the summer heat and through a desert, marching day and night, stopping only at noon to rest during the high temperature. Although many of his men dropped out exhausted, Alexander did not stop the chase. According to him, that march was supposed to be easy for his men who had walked so many snows, crossed so many rivers, and traversed so many mountain ranges. Even the sea that covered the road with tides or the narrow pass of Cilicia could not stop their advance.

Soon after Bessus betrayed and murdered Darius, Alexander started the pursuit of Bessus and his supporters. Bessus had declared himself king of Asia and successor to Darius, and he did his best to prevent Alexander from moving on farther, destroying all crops before the Macedonians so they would lack supplies and have to stop the chase. Bessus' efforts, however, did not halt Alexander and his people. They kept advancing notwithstanding deprivation, snow, wide rivers, and many other obstacles. Many Macedonian horses died during those marches, and some soldiers, no longer in shape for service, were sent home. At last, Alexander's relentless persecution paid off; he captured Bessus and ordered his execution for the betrayal and murder of Darius.

Alexander was a remarkable besieger. He was undisputedly the best in ancient history and perhaps the best ever. Every—until then—invulnerable city, eventually fell under the persistence of his attacks. Even those enemies who initially laughed at his harmless attempts to capture their impregnable towns, like the people of Aornos, ultimately capitulated. His persistence helped him capture the legendary rock of Aornos. The relentless press of the Macedonians, moving up troop by troop, persevering with a stubborn siege, finally wore down the defenders and caused them to abandon the rock.

Typically, Alexander would persist with a siege until the defenders lost all hope of saving their city. If repelled by a powerful resistance, he would attack again, and again, replacing exhausted companies with fresh ones, until he could dictate his terms. Alexander's energy surpassed that of his generals and soldiers. His valor, as Coenus said, was always increasing while the energy of his soldiers was gradually running out. Nothing stopped the young conqueror—not the distances, inclemency, or the enemies.

On Being Proactive

Good leaders have an inclination to action that helps them get things done and produce above-normal results. The high-scoring ice hockey player Wayne Gretzky said that we miss 100 percent of the shots we don't take.[7] Proactive leaders create and shape circumstances, rather than being shaped by them; they take the initiative more than others do. Those leaders take full responsibility for the results of their own actions, as well as for the actions of their teams. Reactive leaders, on the other hand, are more frequently at the mercy of circumstances and likely to blame them for their misfortunes.

Alexander was proactive. If something was not working as he wished, Alexander would take the initiative and do things personally. That gave a message to the people in charge of important projects, and as a result, the proactive environment spilled down the chain of command, reaching every unit of Alexander's army.

Alexander always advanced toward new objectives, knowing that his power and reputation increased more during battles than in quiet periods. He was a relentless hard worker who took the initiative and the responsibility to make things happen, and so were the members of his team.

Focus

Being proactive does not mean to attempt everything possible. "No country," said Henry A. Kissinger, "can act wisely simultaneously in every part of the globe at every moment of time."[8] Let us recall what Michael Porter said about strategy: "Strategy is making trade-offs in competing. The essence of strategy is deciding what *not* to do."[9] No one has unlimited resources. Alexander, in particular, had very limited resources when he departed from Macedonia to conquer the world.

Alexander concentrated his resources on the task at hand, and only when the task was finished would he focus his efforts on another objective. He would typically gather all his siege engines, engineers, foot soldiers, cavalry, ships, and allies' forces and put them to work together, focused on the objective in front of them, attacking by several means at once until the opponent capitulated.

Alexander's focalized activities were not limited to battles, but they were rather his style of management. After conquering Miletus, for example, Alexander dismissed most of his combat ships, keeping just a few cargo ships to transport troops and redeploying the marines and the money saved to more productive land operations.

Instead of diverting efforts by attacking various small targets, Alexander preferred to center his crusades on vital cities, leaving the easier task of pacifying satellite communities to future governors. He believed that the greater the obstacle, the more essential it was to overcome it. The task in front of Alexander became his obsession until it was finished.

Finishing Work

Few things are more discouraging than to work hard and to find out eventually that the effort was in vain—just because the task was not properly finished. As long as a wild element remains, a campaign is not completely finished. Great generals of history recognized that giving their opponents the chance to recover could be pernicious for them, especially if their opponents had learned their strengths and weaknesses. "If you start to take Vienna," said Napoleon Bonaparte, "take Vienna." He added that you must not fight too often with one enemy, or you will teach your enemy all your art of war.[10]

Alexander stated the concept of finishing work in these words:

If I believed that our grip on the lands we have so swiftly conquered were sufficiently firm, I would certainly break loose from here.[11]

He went on to say:

But our empire is new and, if we are prepared to admit the truth, insecure; the barbarians still hold their necks stiff beneath the yoke.[12]

And finally he added,

We must either let go what we have taken or seize what we do not yet hold. Men, surgeons who treat sick bodies leave behind noth-

ing that will harm the patient; just so we must cut away whatever
is an obstacle to our rule. A small spark overlooked often starts
a big fire. Where the enemy is concerned, nothing can be safely
underestimated.[13]

To emphasize the importance of finishing a campaign, many times Alexander got personally involved in these final matters. When the Mardians omitted sending emissaries to surrender to Alexander, as other Hyrcanian cities had done, he refused to continue his march. He left the luggage behind, and taking a light army with him, he went after the rebels. The task demanded a great effort because the locals hid in dense vegetation to ambush the Macedonians, but Alexander hunted the Mardians relentlessly until they lost all hope and capitulated.

Shortly after Alexander seized Cyropolis in the year 329 B.C., the Bactrians rebelled against Macedonia, and the Scythians started to become an additional threat as well. The timing could not have been worse as Alexander had still not recovered from a serious wound in his neck. He had problems speaking and could not ride a horse.

Alexander believed that delaying the war until he was fully recovered would only make his enemies stronger, and he felt powerless knowing that his people would not want him to attack, given the circumstances. When he addressed his soldiers to convince them that he had recovered enough to start the fight, his voice was so feeble that even the people near him had trouble hearing him. Furthermore, the visionary Aristander had told him initially that the omens were adverse; but after being pushed by Alexander, the visionary changed his interpretation of the portents.

The unfortunate series of events continued. The king received the bad news that Spitamenes, the instigator of the Bactrian rebellion, had surprised Menedemus in an ambuscade. Spitamenes had killed numerous soldiers and was aiming to starve others by besieging them. The next morning, Alexander, moved more by pride than by physical strength, put on his body armor, walked out of his tent, and stood up in front of his soldiers. It was the first time he had done that since being wounded in Cyropolis. His men looked up to him so much that his presence alone was sufficient to inspire them. They responded cheerily, with tears in their eyes, and agreed with Alexander's desire to continue the campaign—although he was not fully recovered.

Immediately, Alexander started to prepare to cross the river Tanais. Before the crossing, Scythian emissaries came to him and asked him to reconsider his attack, offering instead their friendship while keeping their independence. "Had the gods willed that your stature should match your greed," they said to Alexander, "the world could not hold you. You would touch the east with one hand and the west with the other, and reaching the west you would want to know where the mighty god's light lay hidden." Later they added, "Just cross the Tanais and you will discover the extent of Scythian territory—but you'll never catch the Scythians."[14] The king disregarded their threats, dismissed them, and started the crossing.

He ordered his men to direct the rafts toward the opposite shore, and the Scythians responded by placing their cavalry upon that shore to avert the landing of the Macedonian rafts. In addition to the Scythians throwing arrows from the opposite coast, the Macedonians had to deal with the problem of maintaining a direct course, for the current of the river was impeding them. The Macedonians could not throw missiles from the unstable rafts, but they found the catapults to be a very effective alternative to harm the enemy on the shore.

As soon as the rafts landed, Macedonians and their allies became efficient again at throwing their lances. Alexander was still feeble, but he compensated for his physical weakness with incredible courage. His soldiers were unable to hear his words of encouragement because his voice was too weak, but they could see him fighting with bravery. They encouraged each other and charged relentlessly against the enemy. The Scythians could not resist the violent attack for long, and they gradually gave up ground.

When they finally fled, Alexander chased them for a while; but he started to lose consciousness and had to stop. He instructed his men, however, to continue with the pursuit until the sunset. They returned around midnight having killed and captured a great number of Scythians. Asians had believed the Scythians to be invincible; therefore, the news of Alexander's stunning victory, leading his troops while physically impaired, helped him to subjugate the rebellious territories of Asia.

Chapter XIV

Managing Incentives

"Call it what you will, incentives are what get people to work harder."

Nikita Khrushchev[1]

REWARD AND COERCIVE power are two of the five sources of power proposed by French and Rave.[2] Reward power is based on an individual's ability to recompense. People comply with the leader because of a desire for reward. In contrast, coercive power is based on an individual's capacity to punish. People comply with the leader due to fear of penalization.

These two sources of power depend on the organization or group because they are related to the individual's position in it. Reward power and especially coercive power tend to induce lower levels of loyalty than expert and referent power.[3] They are more likely to generate compliance or resistance reactions among followers, rather than commitment[4]. Alexander's use—and abuse—of reward and coercive power increased with his overwhelming success.

Reward Power

"The reward of one duty," said the British writer George Eliot, "is the power to fulfill another."[5] Good leaders should remain alert to the need for recognition and reward those who perform excellent jobs, especially those who work below the radar and do not receive adequate compensation for their work. The team spirit of followers will be negatively affected without proper recognition and reward, and they may end up lowering their performance or leaving the organization. The reward does not need to be a material possession; it could as well be an emotional or intangible reward. A combination of tangible and intangible rewards is frequently a wise choice.

Alexander paid close attention to incentives and meritocracy, making sure that loyalty and superb behavior were generously rewarded within the scope of his initially limited resources. Because he considered the safety of his people a priority, he was inclined to recompense those who contributed to it. Conversely, from the beginnings of his reign he showed, with words and deeds, his lack of patience with under-performers. He was mercilessness with traitors. As time elapsed and greater success smiled on the Macedonians, Alexander distributed treasures among his soldiers and their families. Whether in the midst of their most productive years or retiring, brave soldiers consistently received the proceeds of their collective effort.

Alexander made sure that his brave casualties had a noble death, were buried as heroes, and remembered in Macedonia with bronze statues. Their relatives received money, pensions, tax exemptions, and honors. Top commanders' funerals were splendid when circumstances allowed. From time to time, he released contingents of exhausted soldiers, letting them go back to their families and replacing them with new fresh troops. Those who went back to Macedonia and to other allied nations as war veterans encouraged younger soldiers to join Alexander's army. Released allied contingents received the payment agreed upon, and normally an additional payment for consistent good performance. Also before soldiers returned to their homes, Alexander released them from their debts.

As for the soldiers still fighting by Alexander's side, words of encouragement and exceptional rewards were always available for outstanding work. Those special rewards ranged from money to promotion to higher ranks, to power and responsibilities in Alexander's ever-growing empire. He made them feel like owners of the conquered territories. Alexander awarded golden circlets to brave soldiers as a symbol of his recognition of their courage.

Overall, Alexander made sure that those who stayed in his ranks were the envy of anyone else—no longer poor and unknown but rich and full of glory. He said that his first pleasure in life was to pay back all the brave soldiers who deserved it. Because of his generosity, those Macedonians at home and many soldiers from various nations wanted to be part of that glorious army and participate in its dangerous adventures.

Alexander's opponents, who instead of fighting him surrendered unconditionally, were likely to earn his trust. On many occasions, he awarded them territories to govern—sometimes even larger than the original ones they ruled. Frequently, he gave those who had yielded to him the territory of those who had persisted in their insurrection. Similarly, Alexander enlisted a good number of former opponents and even entrusted some of them with the command of troops.

Alexander's goodwill toward those who surrendered to him, in addition to his ruthlessness with the rebellious, encouraged the governors of some nations to join him rather than trying to fight him, and gave the inhabitants of those countries a reason to cultivate his friendship. Alexander divided people into two categories: friends and foes. He did not accept neutrality—the Romans would do the same in the future. Anyone neutral had to take a side, and if they did not, he would consider them foes.

This young king assigned the most important projects, as in the parable of the talents (Matthew 25:21): "Well done, good and faithful servant; you were faithful over a few things, I will make you ruler over many things."[6] He did not hesitate to thank and congratulate Persian and other nations' troops that joined the various Macedonian units, either as soldiers or as commanders, for their commitment and performance.

One of the most important rewards given by Alexander to his best people was the opportunity to grow, almost without limits.

Alexander was a magnet for success, and every endeavor he undertook eventually finished victoriously. The riches of Alexander's soldiers vanished with their demises; their glory, however, lasted forever. The extent of Alexander's generosity to his good soldiers, caused his mother Olympia to write him a letter where she acknowledged his magnanimity in enriching his people, but she suggested that he moderate those rewards and honors. In her opinion, Alexander was making his people equal to kings, giving them power and the opportunity to make their own friends, while he remained poor.

In the initial years of his crusade, Alexander was approachable and unostentatious, making himself like his common soldiers and rejecting the pride and honors of his royal heritage. The emotional bond between Alexander and his people was the envy of many armies. His people's love of him became more evident during difficult times as Alexander was always ready to support and grieve for his people.

Alexander considered monetary incentives as secondary to rewards like honors, encouragement, or promotion. Nevertheless, he was careful to establish different levels of rewards based on accomplishments. For instance, the first person to reach the summit of an enemy's cliff would receive ten talents, the second nine, and so on. In order to promote teamwork and cohesion Alexander also established compensation for units and for the overall army—also based on performance.

Many reward systems have been discussed in the past decades. Perhaps the ultimate best practice model, according to Jeremy

Hope and Robin Fraser from the University of California at Berkeley, should have three elements. A percentage of rewards based on the relative success of the company (the Wallander approach), a percentage based on the relative success of the local team (the Descarpentries approach), and an element based on personal merit (unrelated to specific targets).[7]

Coercive Power

Among all the sources of power, coercive power is the most likely to have a negative impact. Potential reactions to this source of power include resistance and compliance. Commitment, on the other hand, would be very unlikely. As Afsaneh Nahavandi wrote in *The Art and Science of Leadership*, "Once the access to rewards or punishment is taken away by the organization, a leader or individual who is relying on such sources loses power."[8] Alexander, however, used this power source to a large—sometimes exaggerated—degree.

In 335 B.C., the city of Thebes witnessed and suffered the first major demonstration of Alexander's coercive power. The insurrection of this city encouraged other Greek cities, including Athens, which taking advantage of the situation, changed its neutral position and called for a Hellenic crusade against Macedonia. The Athenians started to negotiate an alliance with the Persian king.

Alexander decided to eliminate the Greek revolution. He headed directly to Thebes, covering 200 miles in fourteen days, mostly through mountains and hills. He expected the Thebans to send him ambassadors to negotiate a peace treaty and to surrender, but that did not happen.

Alexander razed the city to the ground. With the annihilation of Thebes, Alexander showed the Greeks and warned the Persians that he was anything but weak. This terrifying example of coercive power brought Greece into submission, and at the same time, gratified those allies who had remained loyal to Macedonia—Phocians, Plataeans, and Boeotians. Other leaders later applied this type of severe punishment, including Napoleon Bonaparte who believed "The act of policing is, in order to punish less often, to punish more severely."[9]

Alexander applied similar punishment, albeit in different degrees, to other rebellious cities like Tyre and Gaza (narrated previously in this book).

He promptly and severely punished conquered cities for revolts to serve as an example and to keep other towns in line. He usually executed those who led or participated in such revolts and sometimes razed their cities. By tackling revolts immediately, he stopped them from spreading.

While clearly questionable from a humanitarian standpoint, Alexander's use of coercive power saved the Macedonians many battles and helped them prevent many uprisings. While leaving Perga, Alexander received diplomats from the city of Aspendus who offered their submission and kindly requested him not to place a garrison inside their town. He agreed to the petition, but in exchange demanded that Aspendus pay fifty talents—a significant amount for that city—and turn in all its horses, which was in turn agreed to by the diplomats.

Soon after Alexander moved on, however, the people of Aspendus breached the agreement, refusing to make the settled payments and locking themselves inside the city walls, leaving the Macedonian garrison outside. As soon as Alexander received the bad news, he returned to Aspendus. The sole presence of an angry Alexander and his army surrounding the city terrified the defenders, who sent emissaries begging that they reestablish peace on the original terms. Although Alexander was not prepared for a long siege, he refused the proposal. Instead, he demanded that Aspendus double its payment, yield their leaders as hostages, pay an annual tribute to Macedonia, and accept a governor named by him. Fearing Alexander's punishment, the people of Aspendus complied with all of his requirements.

At the time when Alexander was fighting the Mardians, his enemies unexpectedly captured his beloved horse Bucephalus. This horse did not allow any person other than the king to ride it, and it would bend its knees for Alexander to mount it. When Alexander found out about its kidnapping, he sent an ultimatum saying that no Mardian would be left alive if he did not get his horse back. The Mardians, knowing Alexander's history of using coercive power, sent him not only the horse but also gifts to appease him.

Plots against kings' lives were common in ancient history. Successors who craved access to the throne and enemies who preferred to face a weaker leader represented continuous threats to the lives of governors and kings. When menaces were likely to materialize, Alexander acted preemptively, making ruthless examples of those who contemplated killing him.

Even though Alexander relied on a group of friends to hear and judge suspects, defendants' rights were almost unknown in those times when interrogation methods included torture. Conclusive evidence, as we know it today, was often impossible to obtain. It is difficult to conclude whether the king and his friends were right or wrong in deciding to execute his friends Philotas and Callisthenes, suspects in two different plots against his life.

Alexander despised those who betrayed and murdered other kings as well, perhaps thinking that they would do the same to him if they had the chance. He arrested and executed all those who had participated in the treachery to Darius. Bessus, who had murdered Darius and assumed power in his place, was captured and, at Alexander's request, brought to him stripped of his clothes and in a dog collar. "What bestial madness possessed you," Alexander asked Bessus, "that you should dare to imprison and then murder a king from whom you had received exemplary treatment? Yes, and you rewarded yourself for this treachery with the title of king which was not yours."[10] After a severe punishment, Bessus was finally sent to Bactra, capital of Bactria, for execution.

Alexander also despised Greek mercenaries who had fought for other countries against their own compatriots, thus infringing on the League of Corinth's resolution, and was ready to penalize them. He believed that Greek soldiers who fought against their own nation were not much better than criminals. After the Battle of Gaugamela, those Greek mercenaries who had fought for the Persians and did not die fighting were sent in chains to Macedonia to do hard labor.

The king applied coercive power to those who had committed crimes against his people and his predecessors, doing everything possible to avenge those crimes, even if they had occurred long ago. He was eager to punish Darius for various crimes, including the hiring of the assassin of his father Philip II of Macedon. He wanted to punish Persia for the invasion by Darius' ancestors of Macedonia and Greece, as well as for sending soldiers to Thrace, which was under Macedonian domain.

As the victorious young king of Macedonia was approaching Persepolis in 330 B.C., he encountered a group of 4,000 Greek POWs, whom the Persians had released now that Alexander had defeated Darius for the second time and was coming to the city. The captors of these unfortunate Greek POWs had mutilated and tortured them. Some had had their hands cut off, others their feet or their ears. Alexander and his soldiers were shocked. They wept contemplating the POWs' hapless appearance and listening to their experiences of torture. Alexander promised to send these Greek captives back to their cities and gave them significant money and gifts.

As for Persepolis, he considered this old capital of Persia as the most detestable city to Greeks and Macedonians. For that reason, the punishment was about to be brutal. Alexander would not accept surrender or treasures from this opulent city, as he did from other cities, but instead he was determined to demolish it, both as an example to others and to appease the desire for revenge of

Greeks and Macedonians. Many inhabitants of Persepolis left before Alexander arrived, and those who stayed were killed until he ordered the massacre to stop. His soldiers razed the city, captured its incalculable riches and, following their drunken king, burned its magnificent palace, which had been the home of many kings.

Later, Alexander regretted part of his actions and said that a harder punishment for the Persians would have been to keep the palace, so they would have had to see him occupying the throne of Xerxes, the Great king of Persia who reigned from 486 B.C. to 465 B.C.

Alexander also used reward and coercive power when assessing administrators of annexed territories and treasuries. He was watchful of mismanagement, quick to remove those who did not perform well, and inclined to entrust the best administrators with additional resources and responsibilities. Tyrannical governors were put on trial, and if convicted, often executed. Nevertheless, he was careful to find out the truth about suspicious managers before making any final decision. In most cases, he would hide his anger and treat the suspects normally, letting them keep their ranks until he could study the reports about them. As word of his anger against those officials who had committed serious offenses spread, many of them recalled illegal or arbitrary acts.

Alexander's tolerance declined as the world steadily bowed to him, and his use of coercive power, which is questionable per se, sometimes degenerated into abuse of it. Punishments applied by Alexander and his people, however, were usual some twenty-two centuries ago.

Chapter XV

Other Leadership and Strategy Lessons

"Far better to dare mighty things, to win glorious triumphs, even
though checkered by failure, than to take rank with those poor spir-
its who neither enjoy much nor suffer much, because they live in
the gray twilight that knows not victory, nor defeat."[1]

Theodore Roosevelt

Bold Decisions

"STRONG LEADERS WILLING to make choices," says Michael Porter, "are essential."[2] Alexander was one of those—a leader
who did not tremble when making a tough decision under pressure, and a leader who listened to others before making an important choice and took responsibility for the consequences of
his decisions.

When he succeeded his father to the throne of Macedonia, his fist bold decision was to retain the control of Greece by use of force, against the advice of his generals. He decided not only to subdue Greece, but also to conquer the world with his small army.

In spite of the high risks involved and against the advice of his engineers, who believed that the height of the mound where Gaza was located made it impossible to attack the town, Alexander determined that Gaza should be taken over. He stood firm behind his decision and took the responsibility for his choice, which eventually ended in a remarkable victory.

Alexander made bold choices in many other circumstances. At Granicus, he disregarded the advice of Parmenio, who warned that an immediate attack would jeopardize the entire campaign. At Miletus, he first made the smart decision of not engaging in a naval battle against the Persians. After the successful conquest of this town, he decided to dismiss most of his battle ships, redeploying the marines and the money saved. Some believed that he intended this last action to deprive his soldiers of their desire for returning. Aiming to rule the world and not just a part of it, he decided to reject Darius' peace proposals—twice. All these daring decisions finally paid off.

Napoleon Bonaparte said that nothing is more difficult, and therefore more precious, than to be able to decide.[3] Alexander made countless bold decisions during combats, on the spot and under extreme pressure. Even though not all of them were perfect and a few were mistaken, the fact that Alexander did not lose any single battle speaks for itself. "Fortune," as proclaimed the Roman poet Virgil (70-19 B.C.), "favors the bold."[4]

Confronting Obstacles

From a very young age, Alexander was taught that problems should be faced, not avoided. His mother Olympia made sure that he learned about sacrifice, despite being a prince, and his father Philip II assigned him early responsibilities as regent of Macedonia. Alexander had to cope with many obstacles during his life, and not all of them were the result of his campaigns.

He was short for a warrior, albeit tough and full of energy, in times when most civilizations equaled physical size and strength with power and leadership. Even after he proved his extraordinary qualities, some enemies, like the Scythians, were surprised when they met him personally, for they judged a man's courage depending on his physical appearance, and they found Alexander's physique inconsistent with his reputation.

When his reign began, he faced all kinds of obstacles and perils. He was young and inexperienced, a contested heir to Philip's throne with enemies in Greece, Persia, and even in Macedonia. Alexander's army and resources were insignificant compared to those of some of his opponents. As a result, he had to overcome extreme and diverse difficulties during his battles, including the challenge to defend his soldiers from flank attacks and encircling maneuvers. By fighting always in foreign territories, he was under disadvantages in terms of geographical intelligence, threats of ambushes, and lack of supplies. Wide rivers, steep mountains, hostile animals and insects, long deserts, snow, and vast distances were some of the numerous obstacles that Mother Nature threw at Alexander and his people's advance. The absence of maps in those days complicated even more Alexander's worldwide crusade, jeopardizing sometimes the results of the campaign, as was the case when he landed on an unexpected island during his battle against Porus.

The virtual invulnerability of many cities, and their ability to resist for long periods without supplies—sometimes years—represented a huge obstacle to the ambitions of the Macedonian conqueror. Besides, carrying siege engines was laborious, sometimes not even possible because of the nature of the terrain, and he could not afford to lose much time on each city if he wanted to conquer the world. Only his relentless determination, combined with the maximum use of his resources and strategies, allowed him to overcome these obstacles. Among others, the grueling captures of Tyre and Gaza in only ten months were achievements that no other general in ancient history had accomplished.

Adaptability

A good leader must be able to adapt and reinvent when circumstances require it. "Change before you have to,"[5] was one of the lessons taught by the former CEO of General Electric, Jack Welch. While Alexander did not compromise his goals and principles, he showed enviable speed and flexibility. He quickly modified his tactics to accommodate new conditions.

During battles, where the game of military chess sometimes altered drastically in a moment, Alexander was particularly alert to actual and potential changes. He redeployed resources, sending the units better suited for the circumstances. His precise assessments and fast responses were determinant to surviving and winning numerous battles.

Not only in combat was Alexander quick to spot changes and adapt to them. Accustomed to dealing with the unexpected, he modified plans without hesitation to respond to political events, rebellions, and other situations that could influence the future of his crusade. "Change is the law of life," said John F. Kennedy, "and those who look only to the past or present are certain to miss the future."[6]

Money Matters

Although Alexander considered monetary incentives secondary to other forms of rewards—like honors, encouragement or promotion—he was aware of their crucial importance in a worldwide campaign. For each battle or siege, he would designate a person to take possession of the enemy's treasuries, baggage, horses, elephants, pack animals, and any other valuable resources. The main job of that person, usually of a high rank, was to make sure the enemy, in its retreat, did not escape with its riches.

Typically, Alexander assigned a section of the Macedonian heavy infantry to guard the treasures that he carried with him in his advance. This section would not participate in fights unless it was attacked. Other treasures of Alexander's empire remained for safekeeping with guards at different cities.

Among the most significant treasuries were those assembled at Susa, where he got 50,000 talents of silver and other valuable possessions that a series of Persian kings had accumulated over a long time, at Persepolis—about 120,000 talents—and at Ecbatana, where Parmenio collected 180,000 talents and delivered it to Harpalus for safekeeping.

The Value of Information

Knowledge is power. Alexander had high regard for the acquisition and control of sensitive information—like war tactics, alliances, and strategic plans. His efforts to keep important information secret became evident when he reproached Aristotle for publishing books that revealed the uncommon knowledge that he and his close friends had received directly from the philosopher. He wrote the following letter to the master:

> *Alexander to Aristotle, greetings. You have not done well to publish your books of oral doctrine; for what is there now that we excel others in, if those things which we have been particularly instructed in be laid open to all? For my part, I assure you, I had rather excel others in the knowledge of what is excellent, than in the extent of my power and dominion. Farewell.*[7]

As Professor Jeffrey Pfeffer (Stanford University) argues in his book *Managing with Power,* "There is little doubt that information, and the certainty that it can provide, is a source of power."[8]

Religious Faith

From a young age, Alexander believed that he had been chosen by the gods to become the master of the world; such a belief—which gradually became an obsession—propelled his energy and strengthened his ambition. He offered regular sacrifices to Greek gods, and at times to local gods, in gratitude for their help in his campaigns. He used to invoke the protection of deities before important events—especially battles. The prophet Aristander would lead Alexander in prayers as the king requested the assistance of the gods.

To get the favor of deities, Alexander would not miss any opportunity to offer them sacrifices, presents, altars, and parades. In addition to their religious significance, rites proved very efficient in calming the fears among his troops, as on the night before the Battle of Gaugamela, when troops were terrified by the massive number of soldiers that Darius had gathered, knowing that, in the best-case scenario, a good number of Macedonians and allies would die in the battlefield.

Alexander was aware of the great influence that religion had over the masses and shared Plato's idea that people are twice armed if they fight with faith. He put questions to oracles and apparently received very encouraging answers. The dissemination of those replies increased the hope and confidence among his soldiers.

Alexander held in high regard the interpretations of the oracles and prophets, particularly of Aristander, and was watchful of their warnings. As a person of faith, he respected traditional observances of foreign deities, and even when he was near death, he refused to abandon his religious duties and asked to be carried out on his bed to perform his regular spiritual activities.

Good Fortune

Journalist and broadcaster Larry King says that those who have succeeded at anything and don't mention luck are kidding themselves.[9] Not everybody, however, gives the same credit to fortune. In fact, opinions about it are very diverse. Some people, like Thomas Jefferson, are great believers in luck and find that the harder they work the more they have of it.[10] Some others believe that good luck is a matter of seizing opportunities. Using William Shakespeare's words, they believe that "there is a tide in the affairs of men which, taken at the flood, leads on to fortune."[11] Those who are more skeptical, like the American writer Bret Harte—who wrote about the California gold rush—believe that the only sure thing about luck is that it will change.[12]

Alexander preferred to attribute his good fortune, which was considerable, to the assistance of the gods, claiming that divine favor, rather than good luck, backed him. For those who do not believe in luck at all, it will be hard to explain many fortunate circumstances of Alexander's life, including the few described below, which eventually contributed to his unparalleled success.

Several times Alexander looked at death, yet did not die. A combination of good skills, good luck, and good soldiers kept him alive. During the Battle of Granicus, for instance, Cleitus saved his life. In the battle against the Mallians, Peucestas, Abreas, and Leonnatus protected the Macedonian king and saved his life with their own bodies.

An important blessing for Alexander was the death of the remarkable Persian commander Memnon of Rhodes. Originally a Greek general, Memnon had extensive knowledge of Persia and Macedonia and represented an obstacle to Alexander's plans in Asia Minor. After his death, the Persians could not find a commander of similar caliber to oppose the advance of the Macedonians.

When Alexander was marching toward Cilicia and Phoenicia at the beginning of the year 333 B.C., he needed to pass through the treacherous seashore of Pamphylia, but the route was very dangerous during southerly winds, for the violent waves crashing into the sheer cliffs made the passage deadly. Before the Macedonians started their march toward Cilicia and Phoenicia, the southerly winds had been hard and persistent. As the Macedonians arrived at the beach, however, the wind suddenly turned north, making the advance simple. Alexander and his troops attributed this fortunate episode to the grace of the gods.

Later during that same year, in November 333 B.C., before the Battle of Issus, Alexander, who wanted this fight to take place in a narrow place, led his troops toward Issus, and stopped there to decide whether they should move forward or wait for reinforcements from Macedonia. The place was ideal for a fight, as the narrow corridor would make both forces almost equal in the front line.

A combination of factors, including Alexander's sound planning and strategy, but also good fortune, caused Darius to leave the open ground and go into a confined space. In his customary speech to his people right before the battle, Alexander claimed that the gods had already started to help them by suggesting Darius fight in the narrows. Most soldiers in Alexander's lines took that as a divine endorsement, crucial to motivate them in a battle where they were severely outnumbered by the enemy.

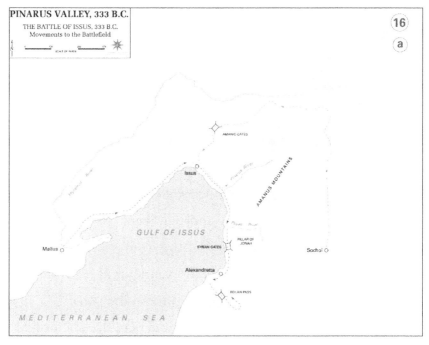

Fig. 16. Courtesy of the Department of History, United States Military Academy.

Darius believed that Alexander had been lucky in his initial campaigns and that fortune would eventually favor the Persians. It did not happen that way.

More than a year later, in Egypt, a mistake of his guides in choosing routes left his army for a long time at the mercy of a sandstorm in the desert. Their provisions were almost finished when a providential storm saved them.

Not only Alexander's cautiousness to scout the terrain ahead and prevent ambushes, but also his unceasing good fortune, saved his army from deadly attacks during vulnerable times. They were not attacked, for instance, as they were making the difficult crossing of the Tigris River, before the Battle of Gaugamela.

Similar good fortune delivered the king from a conspiracy against his life, when a longer than usual banquet and an eccentric woman, followed by a repented conspirator, saved him from a deadly plot.

Chapter XVI

Mistakes

"The essence of government is power; and power, lodged as it must be in human hands, will ever be liable to abuse."[1]

James Madison

B ILL CLINTON SAID that everybody makes mistakes while president.[2] Although Alexander was a unique leader with various extraordinary qualities, he made mistakes. His errors included abuse of power, excessive drinking, taking unnecessary risks, and making tactical miscalculations. For a long time, Alexander exceeded all previous kings in terms of clemency and self-control, but he failed to maintain that degree of moderation to the end of his life, when his success and power reached their peak.

Abuse of Power

Plato, the mentor of Alexander's mentor, favored the idea of a totalitarian state. Alexander liked this idea, but mostly because he wanted to be the ruler of a huge state: the world.

Alexander's eventual abuses in his later life led him to unnecessary destruction, like the demolition of the royal palace of Persepolis. Cruel punishments and reverence requirements, a practice introduced by the conquered Persian soldiers, caused resentment among some of his soldiers and friends, especially Callisthenes. Also, to avoid a plot against his life, or because he did not want any other person to have the same power that he had, Alexander did not name a successor, even when he was about to die from fever (presumably caused by malaria). When asked to name his successor, Alexander replied *the best man*, setting the ground for internal fights and for the division of his empire after his death.

Exhausted with the interminable campaign, beyond the frontiers of the known world, his soldiers finally cried out for rest. Coenus, representing the soldiers, expressed it in the following words:

> *By your magnificent achievements, Your Majesty, you have triumphed not over your enemies alone but over your own soldiers, too. Whatever mortals were capable of, we have achieved. We have crossed lands and seas, all of them now better known to us than to their inhabitants. We stand almost at the end of the earth; you are preparing to enter another world and you seek an India even the Indians do not know.*[3]

Coenus went on saying:

Look at our bodies—debilitated, pierced with all those wounds, decaying with all their scars! Our weapons are already blunt; our armour is wearing out. We put on Persian dress because our own cannot be brought out to us—we have stooped to wearing the clothes of foreigners! How many of us have a cuirass? Who owns a horse?

And later he added:

Conquerors of all, we lack everything!

Alexander's abuse of power increased the distance between the soldiers and a king who had been very approachable in the past. These later abuses of power, usually combined with his fondness for drink, led him to make a few irreparable mistakes, like the unintended killing of Cleitus, the friend who had saved his life at Granicus, during an argument at a banquet. Also, the torture and killing of Callisthenes and Philotas, suspects of two different conspiracies against Alexander's life, and Philotas' father Parmenio, to prevent retaliation, engendered resentment among Alexander's friends.

"Once we realize that imperfect understanding is the human condition," George Soros, global financier and philanthropist, says, "there is no shame in being wrong, only in failing to correct our mistakes."[4] Alexander acknowledged many of his mistakes, and sometimes tried to correct or to learn form them. He grieved and regretted profoundly some of his irreparable mistakes, like the death of Cleitus, but in later years he never showed the same goodness as in his early years as a king.

Tactical Errors

"Take risks. Ask big questions. Don't be afraid to make mistakes," said David Packard, the co-founder of Hewlett-Packard. "If you don't make mistakes, you're not reaching far enough."[5] Only a few times in his long and extensive campaign did Alexander make tactical errors, none of them important enough to deprive him of a victory. For the Battle of Issus, Alexander had placed few cavalry on his left wing, upon the seashore. Noticing the weakness, Darius recalled the cavalry he had previously sent across the river and redirected most of it to his right to pressure the Macedonian position on the seaside, where the ground was more favorable for his horses.

Alexander recognized his mistake early enough and sent the Thessalian equestrians to his left wing to reinforce the defenses in said area. This last movement, however, weakened his right wing, allowing the possibility of being outflanked by the vast Persian army in that zone; hence, he relocated two squadrons of the Companions from the center to the right wing to solve the problem.

A few times, Alexander's impatience had put him and his people at unnecessary risk. At Granicus, for instance, after the battle was already decided in his favor, his impatience to kill the experienced Greek mercenaries who were retreating cost him many lives. His continuous disregard for death led him also to risk his life, sometimes needlessly.

Mistakes are an eventual and inevitable by-product of getting things done, but avoiding taking risks in order to avoid mistakes is not a wise option. The numbers expressed by late professor Peter Drucker (NYU and Claremont) are questionable, but his argument is compelling: "People who don't take risks generally make about two big mistakes a year. People who do take risks generally make about two big mistakes a year."[6]

Chapter XVII

Alexander's Legacy

"There is nothing impossible to him who will try."[1]

Alexander the Great

An *Impossible* Mission

Now that we have described Alexander's unique qualities in previous chapters, we will go back to the battle that changed the course of the world, the Battle of Gaugamela. The morning of October 1, 331 B.C., King Darius said to his troops, "Today we will consolidate or terminate an empire greater than any age has seen."[2] Darius' selection to assume the throne had been based on his recognized bravery, which far surpassed that of other Persians. He was also a clever strategist.

On the opposite side, Alexander addressed his people, from common soldiers to the highest commanders, with a remarkable and inspiring—yet exaggerated—speech that boosted their spirits and hunger for glory. He reminded his people about their past glories under his command; they had traveled—victorious—vast distances, through many territories, rivers, and mountains, hoping for the decisive fight that they were about to fight. That crucial battle, said the king, was all that remained ahead of them before they returned home.

He reminded them of Granicus, Cilicia, Syria, and Egypt. They had already defeated Darius' commanders at Granicus, and Darius himself at the celebrated Battle of Issus. After that, said Alexander, the Persians had run away and had decided to fight that day only because escape was no longer possible for them.

Aware of the natural human fear of the unknown and unexpected, Alexander told his soldiers not to be worried about the new soldiers that Darius had enrolled—Scythians and Cadusians, among others. The fact that they were unknown, he said, was an indication that they were not very courageous, for great warriors are never unknown. Quite the contrary, everybody knew about Macedonians because of their bravery.

Alexander knew that his people would be shocked to see—and fight—an almost endless Persian army, much larger than the one they had defeated at Issus. Hence, he anticipated the situation, and focused on his army's possible advantages over the Persian one—namely courage and superior weapons. Certainly more soldiers were *standing* on the Persian side, he said, but more were going to be *fighting* on the Macedonian one.[3]

The king reminded his people that he was not asking them to do anything that he would not do himself. He assured his army that he would be fighting, as usual, in the front line, giving the foremost example of bravery, all the wounds covering his body being a proof of it. Finally, he told them that he would reward his soldiers by sharing the huge Persian treasury with them, as was his custom.

Alexander's strategy aimed to tempt an attack of the superior Persian wings to create a gap in the enemy's line. Then, he would break through that gap with the Companion cavalry and attack Darius' position before the Persian flanks could defeat his own troops.

When the Battle of Gaugamela was about to start, Alexander received a report that the Persians had put spears in the battlefield at the place where Darius expected Alexander to send his equestrians. Alexander instructed his generals to avoid the area and told them to warn the cavalry as well. He ordered the front line to advance at an angle to both avoid the spears and to encounter Darius. Darius replied by turning his line at the same angle, intending to charge the left wing of Alexander.

Darius' Scythian equestrians were the first to make contact with the Macedonian front line. Meanwhile, Alexander continued his march to the right until he was almost away from the area that the Persians had evened out before the battle.

Darius had ordered his men to level the ground so that his new weapons, scythe chariots, would be destructive to the Macedonians. Darius knew that as soon as the Macedonians reached an irregular surface, the chariots would be far less effective; therefore, he sent his equestrians to stop the Macedonian advance. Alexander responded by sending Menidas and his cavalry to strike them.

Then the numerous Scythian cavalry joined that combat and forced Menidas to retreat, but Alexander sent the Paeonian contingent to reinforce the area. A fierce combat took place. The Scythian horse cavalry was superior in numbers and better armed than its Macedonian counterparts, and the Macedonians suffered significantly at the beginning, but its continuous charges finally broke the enemy's formation.

Darius now sent the chariots against Alexander, but the Macedonian had already prepared for this maneuver. Once the chariots were within missile range, the Agrianes and Balacrus started to bombard them, causing severe damage to the drivers and horses. Still many chariots reached the Macedonian lines in good shape, but the Macedonians had been previously instructed to intentionally break formation and let them pass through. Nevertheless, the spears and scythes of the chariots killed some Macedonians. Isolated and surrounded by the enemy, the chariots' drivers were defeated when they finally faced the Royal Guard.

Then Darius dispatched the main formation of his army. Alexander sent Aretes against the Persian equestrians to keep them from encircling the Macedonian right. Aretes initially succeeded and even killed the Scythians' leader, but when Darius sent Bactrian units, the Macedonians retreated to the position where Alexander was. In that critical moment, Alexander upbraided and motivated them with determination, and sent them to charge against the enemy once more.

Fig. 17. The charge of the Persian scythed chariots at the Battle of Gaugamela.[1]

The last advance of the Bactrians, however, had made the Persian front line thinner in its right flank. This was exactly the opportunity that Alexander was waiting for, and such a detail did not pass unnoticed by him. He hurried toward the weakened line with the Companions and part of the heavy infantry, and killed numerous Persians with his attack. The Persian left wing managed to move toward Alexander's rear, but the Agrianes equestrians promptly surrounded it. With Alexander himself fighting in the front line of the Macedonian cavalry, and several Persian units separated from their main formation, the Persians suffered many more casualties than the Macedonians and started to give ground.

Alexander was leading his army from a horse—he had exhausted several horses already—and Darius was leading his from a war chariot. Alexander now saw Darius from a distance and advanced toward his archrival. He stabbed many Persians, and the battle gradually turned into a massacre. Darius, seeing only terror around him, turned his chariot and rode away, as did most Persian soldiers in that part of the battlefield. The Macedonians chased the fugitives and killed many of them.

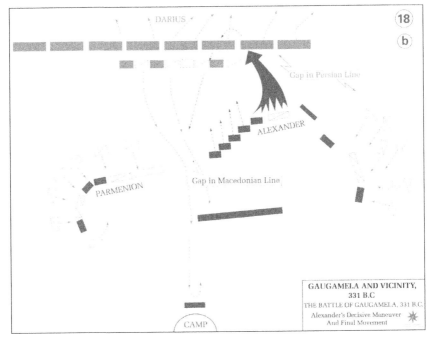

Fig. 18. Courtesy of the Department of History, United States Military Academy.
(Infantry: solid rectangles; cavalry: hollow rectangles)

On the left side, however, the situation was completely different. Parmenio had been surrounded by a larger army led by Mazaeus, and was asking for Alexander's help. For the first time, the Macedonian soldiers were fighting not to win, but just to survive. The Macedonian king was already chasing Darius when he received the bad news of Parmenio's situation. Reluctantly, Alexander stopped the pursuit of his Persian counterpart and returned immediately to help Parmenio. In the meantime, Mazaeus found out about Darius' defeat, and his troops, demoralized, started to relax the pressure against Parmenio. As a result, the Macedonians fighting in that area gradually recovered ground until Mazaeus retreated and escaped, crossing the Tigris River. Parmenio, unaware of his king's fate in the right wing, decided not to chase his enemy.

Alexander was now about to charge the Persian right wing, but his help was not needed anymore. While he was leading a small group of men back to the camp, believing that the entire enemy either had fled or been killed, he ran into a large contingent of the finest Persian cavalry—enhanced by Indian soldiers. Ironically, Alexander faced the most dangerous situation when he had already won the battle.

The Persians stopped initially, but when they realized how small the Macedonian detachment was, they decided to attack them. This fight was perhaps the fiercest of that memorable day. In a risky maneuver, Alexander advanced ahead of his men and killed the leader of the Persian unit first and several other Persians later. The Persians killed several Macedonians too. Alexander lost about sixty Companions, while Hephaestion, Menidas, Coenus, and numerous others suffered wounds.

After a furious battle, the surviving Persians escaped at twilight and Alexander came out victorious. He had shown extraordinary courage and leadership in this last combat, fighting, once more, an enemy that considerably outnumbered his unit.

That single day decided the fortune of an entire era. While the Macedonians had lost only a few hundred men and about 1,000 horses, the Persians' casualties were immense, but more difficult to appraise. This time, Darius had no excuse. With a stunning superiority of numbers, he had chosen the best battlefield to exploit that advantage, and he had elephants and scythe chariots in his lines, which the Macedonians lacked.

Alexander planned the battle masterfully and positioned his troops accordingly, confirming his genius as a strategist and commander. He showed his courage to both armies by fighting in the front line and risking his life more than any other soldier did. That October 1 of 331 B.C., at the age of twenty-five, Alexander started to rule the majority of the known world—an achievement that nobody had equaled in more than 2,000 years. He also became the richest man in the world, and gained the most prominent historical place as a leader and a strategist.

The Great Lessons

Alexander was the most powerful person who ever existed and achieved everything a mortal was capable of achieving. He ruled the known world without limitations. He was the president, the congress, and the supreme court. What is more, he did not inherit such incomparable power from someone else; he built it from an unstable base.

The proverbial and relentless speed of Alexander kept him consistently ahead of his rivals, surprising even those who fought by his side. Such remarkable speed of movement was also revealed in the short time he took to seize the known world, in times when crusades were carried out almost exclusively on foot.

An obsession for long-lasting glory helped him to endure virtually any hardship for the sake of achieving longer-than-life goals. This obsession strengthened his energy and self-confidence, spreading confidence among his people and fear among his enemies.

Alexander's obsession led him to set ambitious, bold, and clear goals for himself and for his people. Owner of a cloudless vision of where he wanted to take his people, Alexander was masterful in communicating and convincing those who would help him to achieve those goals. His convictions about the future had a powerful influence on his followers, making it easier for them to buy into his goals. These excessive goals worked like a self-fulfilling prophesy for him, his soldiers, and his enemies.

A genius in the art of planning, Alexander had an important advantage over his enemies. He analyzed every piece of information, planning as many alternatives as possible. Such perfectionist planning reduced the possibilities of unwanted surprises and led to decisive, swift actions.

The Macedonian king led his people to conquer the world by providing an example. He showed soldiers and enemies his relentless labor and courage. He did not ask from his soldiers anything that he would not do himself. As a result, Macedonians and allies admired him because he was a soldier like them, and in many ways, he was even better than they were. It was difficult for them to complain that something was too dangerous or too demanding when their king himself was doing it.

Knowing his people thoroughly, Alexander developed through time a keen sense of their fears, their problems, and their needs. His timing in inspiring his troops became exquisite, and his words and actions were not doubted. In situations where everyone was expecting the worst, the king's optimism and calmness were contagious. His courage during combat dragged the rest along and spread out among his people like a fire.

Alexander was a charismatic leader. Truly enthusiastic about his revolutionary vision and ideas, he surrounded himself with symbols that built his image. He created a solid emotional bond with his followers, gained a well-deserved touch of historical glamour, and represented the type of leader that every soldier would like to have: courageous, determined, and undefeated.

Aware of the power of reputation, Alexander was very watchful in managing it. He paid special attention to his public appearances; every public act from speeches to religious participations had an objective. "Reputation," he said, "determines military success, and often even a false belief has accomplished as much as the truth."[5] Alexander made sure to rapidly spread the news of his accomplishments to influence undecided key players. The reputation he gained helped him to promote his cause, and in some cases, became a self-fulfilling prophesy.

The initial years of Alexander's reign showed him as a magnanimous and generous leader. His vision of a new world, where each city would keep its culture, religion, currency, laws, and taxes, represented a change in how kings would rule their domains, and his ability to persuade the masses made him dangerous to his enemies. He ended the oligarchic regimes established by the Persians and returned the cities to their original laws with increased democratic and administrative autonomy. Alexander did not want the people that he conquered to regret his victory and believed that those who lived under the same king should have the same rights.

Alexander was extremely sensitive to the cultural differences of diverse nations and realized that varied cultures required different leadership styles. He customized his leadership style to the values and the culture of each nation.

He selected his people very carefully—particularly the Companions who fought around him and helped him make crucial decisions—and empowered them so they could develop their full potential. He was noticeably good at choosing governors, generals, and soldiers. Those he selected and trained saved his life a few times, helped him to achieve his outrageous dreams, and guarded the destiny of his empire until he died.

Alexander developed his superb strategic plans by thinking of his own moves and his opponents' countermoves as if it each battle were a military or political chess game. Before every campaign, he would spend time anticipating his enemies' possible moves and developing strategies to prevent their actions. Not content with identifying and exploiting existing opportunities, he strived to create new ones. The capacity to come up with innovative and unconventional ideas was a hallmark of Alexander, who always seemed to be able to find alternative solutions to problems that represented deadlocks for others.

Alexander used the element of surprise to counterbalance the early disadvantages of his army. He waited for the right timing before acting, concealing the move as much as possible. Once the timing for the action was determined, he acted with speed to maximize the surprise effect on his adversary.

The Macedonian king was willing to negotiate and build strategic alliances, whenever they were possible and convenient for his objectives, but he always kept in mind what alternatives to negotiation he had. He preferred to receive a friendly surrender proposal from his opponents, rather than to spend significant time and resources fighting against each city and country. Yet he was firm in stating and defending the matters that he considered nonnegotiable. Alexander understood that the enemies of his enemies were potential allies of his. He also believed that sharing something, like goals, desire for revenge, lineage, or culture, would better position him to gain the support of other nations. In time, he gained the reputation of a trustworthy individual, which helped him as a negotiator.

In addition to other accomplishments, we remember Alexander for the extreme length and difficulty of his march and for his persistence in besieging impregnable cities. Every city eventually fell under the perseverance of his various attacks. Alexander concentrated his resources on the task at hand. And only when the task was finished, would he focus his efforts on another objective. He was proactive and took the responsibility to make things happen.

Alexander's use of reward and coercive power increased with his success. He paid attention to meritocracy, making sure that he generously rewarded loyalty and superb behavior. He made his people feel like owners of the conquered territories. He assigned the most important projects according to previous merits, regardless of origin. To promote teamwork and cohesion, Alexander also established compensation for units and for the overall army. His goodwill with those who surrendered to him and his cruelty with the rebellious encouraged his adversaries to join him, rather than fight him. Alexander promptly and severely punished conquered cities that revolted, letting them serve as examples and keeping other towns in line.

Alexander did not tremble when making a tough decision under pressure. He listened to others before making an important choice and took responsibility for the consequences of his decisions. From a very young age, he mastered the lesson that problems should be faced, not avoided. He showed speed and flexibility to abandon his comfort zone when needed, modifying his tactics to accommodate new conditions. Alexander had high regard for the acquisition and control of sensitive information—particularly war tactics, alliances, and strategic plans.

As a person of strong faith, Alexander performed his regular spiritual activities and respected traditional observances of foreign deities. He was aware of the great influence that religion had over the masses and attributed his considerable good fortune to the assistance of the gods. Alexander was not a demigod, as he sometimes suggested being, but he certainly showed the confidence of one.

Mistakes are an inevitable consequence of getting things done, and Alexander, who probably did more than any other leader, made mistakes. His errors included abuse of power, excessive drinking, taking unnecessary risks, and making tactical miscalculations. For a long time, he exceeded previous kings in terms of clemency and self-control, but he failed to maintain that degree of moderation to the end of his life, when his success and power reached their peak.

At last, Alexander achieved his dream: he conquered and ruled the known world and gained well-merited everlasting glory. Furthermore, no one has matched his achievements in more than two millennia, and no one is likely to surpass them in the near future. His success, however, as in the case of many other good leaders, had a huge cost. He made incredible sacrifices and, although he did not seem to care, balance was not a highlight of his life. He chose a life of struggle. An example of those sacrifices was described by his officer Coenus when, while standing at the frontier of the known world, he said: "Conquerors of all, we lack everything!"[6]

In spite of his lack of balance, and partially because of it, Alexander's campaigns remain as the ultimate example of leadership and strategy based on a real-life story, never again equaled by any person at any time in history. After his campaigns, virtually all the inhabited world sent envoys with presents to congratulate him, and the few cities where he or his generals had not been, begged for treaties of friendship and alliance with him.

When he was at the peak of his power, early in the morning of June 10, 323 B.C., after ten days of fever seemingly caused by malaria, Alexander closed his eyes forever. His power, however, did not vanish with his death. After the struggle for power that followed Alexander's death, his generals eventually divided his huge empire among more than twenty rulers, and fought over his embalmed body because controlling it meant power and reputation. Ptolemy, ruler of Egypt, seized Alexander's body while it was being carried to Macedonia, and took it to Alexandria, Egypt. For hundreds of years notable leaders, including Roman ruler Julius Caesar, visited Alexander's coffin in Alexandria. So craved was Alexander's presence that his royal clothes *presided* over many of the meetings that his generals held in their respective kingdoms.[7] There was no doubt in those rulers' minds that no human being could ever take his place.

Fig. 19. The Death of Alexander the Great.[8]

Lessons for Current and Prospective Leaders

Alexander lived in a very different age than ours, an age where conquests and warrior-heroes were encouraged. In those times, wars for dominance among nations were customary and well regarded, like competition for market share among business is nowadays. With that caveat in mind, his lessons, from his remarkable good traits and behaviors to his excesses, are numerous and extremely valuable. Those current and prospective leaders who want to capitalize on Alexander's example should not only remember and think carefully about the following lessons, but also put them into practice and master them.

> Set clear and ambitious goals for you and your people. Then communicate those goals with conviction to every member of your team.

> You need to have a passion, or even an obsession, in order to persuade others to follow you. That same passion will help you endure the hardships that you will—certainly—face while pursuing your goals. Your passion and self-confidence will not only inspire your followers, but also will daunt your enemies.

> As a leader, it is your responsibility to develop or reestablish a clear strategy. Do not try to do everything; remember that one of the basics of strategy is deciding what *not* to do.

> Seek to apply proven ideas to current situations, but do not overlook unconventional strategies. Spend significant time thinking of your current and future strategic moves, paying special attention to what your competitors will be doing in the meantime.

> Before entering an undertaking, meditate long and try to foresee what might occur in order to minimize unwanted surprises. Plan for different scenarios, not just for the most likely scenario.

> Pay close attention to details. The sum of small details can make a big difference and tremendous consequences might come from those *little* things. However, do not let your detailed planning end in analysis-paralysis; let it end in bold actions.

➤ Spend time to learn about your opponents and prepare for the unknown by studying how others in the past have coped with similar situations. Before you win, you must prepare to win.

➤ Break down your master plan into smaller milestones. Then plan for each one of them thoroughly, without losing sight of your ultimate goal.

➤ Do not overlook your defensive planning, for your opponents will not just sit there. Be ready to anticipate their moves, react, and adapt.

➤ Listen to different, diverse opinions before making an important decision, but take full responsibility for the consequences of your choices.

➤ Once you have decided your course of action, act fast and try to get the first-mover advantage. Move rapidly and with resolution, setting a fast pace for your entire team. Use your speed—and hard work—to compensate for your shortcomings, particularly when competing against large opponents.

➤ You must execute your plans at the appropriate time, and in some circumstances, delaying your action is the smartest thing to do. Postponing an action, for example, may be a good strategy to surprise or wear out your competitor.

➤ Remain alert and flexible to quickly modify your strategies and accommodate to new conditions. Adapt and reinvent *before* you have to.

➤ Be unpredictable and surprise your competitors by combining speed and secrecy. Determine the right timing for your actions, and then conceal them until you execute them with rapidity to maximize the surprise effect on your competitors.

➤ Lead your people by using one of the most effective leadership tools: providing an example. You need to behave according to the beliefs you preach. Do not ask from your followers anything that you would not do yourself. Be a role model for them. Lead from the front line like Alexander, not behind it like Darius.

➤ Motivate your team with precise, encouraging words and firm actions. Praise their achievements and recognize their strengths. Operate on the emotional and spiritual resources of your people, making them feel like partners in your dream.

➤ Show optimism and confidence, particularly in difficult situations. The harder the circumstances, the tougher you should become.

➤ Confront problems and obstacles promptly. Do not procrastinate or avoid them.

➤ Push the limits. No leader has ever become great without audacity.

➤ Do not underestimate the importance of your reputation because perception does influence reality. Consider beforehand the impact that your words and actions will have on your competitors and your own people. Compose your messages and speeches carefully, paying special attention to your public appearances.

➢ Take time to celebrate victories and share those special moments with your team. Spread the news of your—real—accomplishments to increase your reputation and influence neutral players.

➢ Select your team very carefully, looking for integrity, loyalty, talent, endurance, and courage as the main qualities. Get—and keep—the right people on your team, and get the wrong people off your team.

➢ Empower your subordinates so they can develop their full potential and transform goals into reality. Tell them what they need to achieve rather than how to do it, and get involved only if the situation turns worrisome. Encourage judicious risk taking.

➢ Train your team in the school of hard work and do not let them turn soft or luxurious at work. Prepare them for hardships and crises, until their skills become second nature. Remind them that the fortune of the entire group depends on the performance of each one of them.

➢ Pay close attention to incentives and meritocracy in your organization. Remain alert to the need for recognition and reward of those who perform well, especially those who work below the radar. For them, the reward of one duty is the power to fulfill another.[9]

➢ If you perceive fights or disputes beyond healthy competition in your team, address them fast and condemn them firmly.

➤ Rely more on Referent and Expert power than on Legitimate, Reward, and Coercive power, as the first two tend to cause higher levels of commitment, satisfaction, and performance among followers.[10]

➤ Seek to negotiate and build strategic alliances that can help you achieve your goals. Always keep in mind, however, what alternatives to negotiation you have.

➤ Look for similarities, like a common opponent, with your potential allies and remain sensitive to cultural differences when negotiating with other countries or cultures.

➤ Do not underestimate the importance of information. Knowledge is power. Acquire, control, and keep sensitive information confidential.

➤ Be proactive: create and shape circumstances rather than being shaped by them. Take responsibility for the results of your actions and the actions of your team.

➤ Focus on the project you are undertaking until it is properly finished. If you start to take Vienna, take Vienna.[11] Where your competitors are concerned, do not give them a chance to recover.

➤ Mistakes are an eventual and inevitable by-product of getting things done. Take calculated risks and do not be afraid to make mistakes. Recognize your errors early, correct them, and learn form them. Then move on; do not dwell on your mistakes.

➤ You cannot control luck, but you can increase your odds: the harder you work, the luckier you will get. There are no substitutes for hard work and perseverance. Whenever you have good luck, seize the opportunity.

> If you believe in God, ask for His favor and guidance. Choose your mentors and role models carefully for they will have an effect on your career.

> Be kind to all people, not only to *your* people. Remember Alexander's words: "Possession achieved by the sword is not of long duration, but gratitude for kindness shown is everlasting."[12] Monitor and shake off your arrogance, especially after important achievements.

> Respect other opinions, cultures, races, and religions. Value diversity. Be sensitive to cultural differences among nations and keep in mind that different cultures may require different styles of leadership.

> Preserve your discipline, clemency, and moderation after accomplishing major successes. Keep being an approachable leader. Do not become lavish or excessive, but stay prepared to make additional efforts and endure hardships. Remember that we are what we repeatedly do. Excellence then, is not a single act, but a habit.[13]

The last lesson of this book comes from Alexander (The Great) III of Macedon himself: "Stand firm; for well you know that hardship and danger are the price of glory, and that sweet is the savour [sic] of a life of courage and of deathless renown beyond the grave."[14]

A participant in various conferences and roundtables, including the World Economic Forum, Leandro Martino has been cited in *The Wall Street Journal*, CNN, *Barron's*, Bloomberg, Reuters, Dow Jones, *The Washington Times*, *Business 2.0*, and Yahoo! Finance. A business strategist, the author has researched the life and campaigns of Alexander the Great, as well as the lives of other outstanding leaders, for over a decade. Mr. Martino has an MBA with honors from Columbia University in New York, is a graduate of Harvard University, and holds two master's degrees from international universities. He lives in New York City.

Almost every date of ancient Greece is approximate. Exact dating of events is frequently not possible, as dates tend to vary among authors, depending on the system they used. However, the reader can expect the following dating to be somewhat accurate, with an error of between one or two years in the worst cases.

DATE	EVENT
359 B.C.	Philip II, father of Alexander, ascends the throne of Macedon
July 20, 356 B.C.	Birth of Alexander the Great
343 B.C.	Philip II invites Aristotle to Macedon to educate Alexander
August 336 B.C.	Murder of Philip II of Macedon; accession of Alexander
September 336 B.C.	Murder of Amyntas and Attalus
335 B.C.	Destruction of Thebes
April-June 334 B.C.	Alexander crosses the Hellespont; Granicus Battle
July-August 334 B.C.	Siege of Miletus
Summer 333 B.C.	Alexander in Cilicia and Tarsus
November 333 B.C.	Battle of Issus
January-August, 332 B.C.	Siege of Tyre
September-October 332 B.C.	Siege of Gaza

DATE	EVENT
Winter 332/331 B.C.	Expedition to Siwah in Egypt
Spring 331 B.C.	Foundation of Alexandria in Egypt
Late Spring 331 B.C.	Departure from Egypt
October 1, 331 B.C.	Battle of Gaugamela
November 331 B.C.	Capture of Babylon and Susa
January 330 B.C.	Victory against the Uxians
January-May 330 B.C.	Alexander stays at Persepolis
July 330 B.C.	Death of Darius III
327 B.C.	Capture of the Sogdian Rock
327/326 B.C.	Capture of Aornos
326 B.C.	Alexander at the River Hydaspes; battle with Porus
November 326 B.C.	Start of voyage down the Hydaspes
August 325 B.C.	Alexander starts the return to the west
May 323 B.C.	Alexander falls ill
June 10, 323 B.C.	Death of Alexander

This map shows the known world conquered by Alexander the Great in highlight. The map and the marches are approximations.

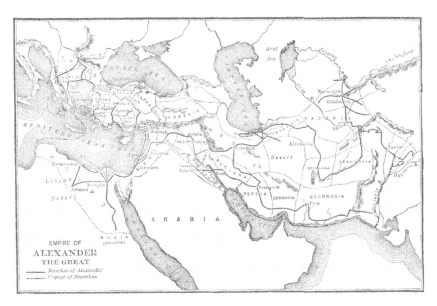

Fig. 20. Empire of Alexander the Great.[1]

NOTES TO CHAPTER I

1 Arrian, *Arrian: The Campaigns of Alexander,* translated by
   Aubrey de Sélincourt, notes by J.R. Hamilton (London:
   Penguin Books, 1958 & 1971), 398.

2 The History Channel, *Julius Caesar's Rome*, A&E Television
   Networks, 2005.

3 Wheeler, Benjamin Ide, *Alexander the Great: The Merging of East
   and West in Universal History* (New York and London: G.P.
   Putnam's Sons, 1900), 1.

4 Arrian, Aubrey de Sélincourt, and J.R. Hamilton, *Arrian: The
   Campaigns of Alexander* (London: Penguin Books, 1958 &
   1971), 160.

5 Gabriel, Richard A. and Karen S. Metz, *A Short History of War:
   The Evolution of Warfare and Weapons*, (Strategic Studies
   Institute, U.S. Army War College, Online version by
   Air War College, 1992), http://www.au.af.mil/au/awc/
   awcgate/gabrmetz/gabr0066.htm.

NOTES TO CHAPTER II

1 BrainyMedia.com, "George S. Patton Quotes," http://www.
   brainyquote.com/quotes/quotes/g/georgespa138200.
   html.

2 Donovan, Brian, 2000, http://en.wikipedia.org/wiki/Image:
   Pella_House_atrium.jpg.

3 French, J.R.P., and B.H. Rave, *The Basis of Social Power*, eds. D. Cartwright and A. Zander, Group Dynamics, 3rd ed., (New York: Harper & Row, 1968).

4 Nahavandi, Afsaneh, *The Art and Science of Leadership* (Upper Saddle River, NJ: Prentice-Hall, Inc., 1997), 77-79.

5 BrainyMedia, "Napoleon Bonaparte Quotes," http://www.brainyquote.com/quotes/quotes/n/napoleonbo139273.html.

6 Dunn, Andrew, Photographer, "Bust of Alexander the Great in the British Museum," (2004), http://www.andrewdunnphoto.com, and http://en.wikipedia.org/wiki/Image:AlexanderTheGreat_Bust.jpg.

NOTES TO CHAPTER III

1 Arrian, Aubrey de Sélincourt, and J. R. Hamilton, *Arrian: The Campaigns of Alexander* (London: Penguin Books, 1958 & 1971), 294.

2 Plutarch, John Dryden, Arthur Hugh Clough, and Victor Davis Hanson, *The Life of Alexander the Great* (New York: The Modern Library, 1992 & 2004), 41.

3 Arrian, Aubrey de Sélincourt, and J. R. Hamilton, *Arrian: The Campaigns of Alexander* (London: Penguin Books, 1958 & 1971), 292-293.

4 Arrian, Aubrey de Sélincourt, and J. R. Hamilton, *Arrian: The Campaigns of Alexander* (London: Penguin Books, 1958 & 1971), 294-295.

5 Reynolds, Siimon, *Thoughts of Chairman Buffett* (New York: HarperCollins, 1998).

6 BrainyMedia, "Aristotle Quotes," http://www.brainyquote.com/ quotes/quotes/a/aristotle145967.html.

7 Public Domain Image, "Aristotle," http://en.wikipedia.org/ wiki/Image:Aristotle.jpg.

8 Plutarch, John Dryden, Arthur Hugh Clough, and Victor Davis Hanson, *The Life of Alexander the Great* (New York: The Modern Library, 1992 & 2004), 7.

9 Plutarch, John Dryden, Arthur Hugh Clough, and Victor Davis Hanson, *The Life of Alexander the Great* (New York: The Modern Library, 1992 & 2004), 8.

10 Public Domain Image, "Alexander the Great Training Bucephalus," http://karenswhimsy.com/alexander-the-great.shtm.

11 Plutarch, John Dryden, Arthur Hugh Clough, and Victor Davis Hanson, *The Life of Alexander the Great* (New York: The Modern Library, 1992 & 2004), 10.

12 Plutarch, John Dryden, Arthur Hugh Clough, and Victor Davis Hanson, *The Life of Alexander the Great* (New York: The Modern Library, 1992 & 2004), 10.

13 Plutarch, John Dryden, Arthur Hugh Clough, and Victor Davis Hanson, *The Life of Alexander the Great* (New York: The Modern Library, 1992 & 2004), 11.

14 French, J.R.P., and B.H. Rave, *The Basis of Social Power,* eds. D. Cartwright and A. Zander, Group Dynamics 3rd ed., (New York: Harper & Row, 1968).

15 Nahavandi, Afsaneh, *The Art and Science of Leadership* (Upper Saddle River, NJ: Prentice-Hall, Inc., 1997), 77-79.

16 Yukl, G. and C. M. Falbe, *The Importance of Different Power Sources in Downward and Lateral Relations* (Journal of Applied Psychology, 1991), 76, 416-423.

NOTES TO CHAPTER IV

1 Collins, James, and Jerry Porras, *Built to Last* (New York: HarperCollins Publishers), 91.

2 BrainyMedia, "Charles De Gaulle Quotes," http://www. brainyquote.com/quotes/quotes/c/charlesdeg144976. html.

3 Porter, Michael E., *What is Strategy?* (Boston, MA: Harvard Business Review, November-December, 1996), 70.

4 Porter, Michael E., *What is Strategy?* (Boston, MA: Harvard Business Review, November-December, 1996), 77.

5 Collins, James, and Jerry Porras, *Built to Last* (New York: HarperCollins Publishers), 94.

6 BrainyMedia, "Rudy Giuliani Quotes," http://www.brainyquote. com/quotes/quotes/r/rudygiulia173443.html.

7 Caratini, Roger, *Alejandro Magno,* translated by Mauro Armiño (Barcelona, Spain: Plaza & Janes Editores, S.A., 1995 & 2000), 150.

8 Arrian, Aubrey de Sélincourt and J.R. Hamilton, *Arrian: The Campaigns of Alexander* (London: Penguin Books, 1958 & 1971), 293.

9 Brown University, Division of Engineering, http://www. engin.brown.edu/courses/en193-194s7/PDFs/engine90-crawford-INTELLECTUAL-PROPERTY2-print.pdf.

NOTES TO CHAPTER V

1 BrainyMedia, "Napoleon Bonaparte Quotes," http://www. brainyquote.com/quotes/quotes/n/napoleonbo143496. html.

2 BrainyMedia, "Bruce Barton Quotes," http://www.brainyquote. com/quotes/quotes/b/brucebarto132397.html.

3 BrainyMedia, "George S. Patton Quotes," http://www. brainyquote.com/quotes/quotes/g/georgespa143495. html.

4 BrainyMedia, "Colin Powell Quotes," http://www.brainyquote. com/quotes/quotes/c/colinpowel144996.html.

5 Inspire21.com http://www.inspire21.com/Images/ ecardTHUMBSx2/willtowin2.jpg.

NOTES TO CHAPTER VI

1 AncientWorlds LLC, "Confucius," http://www.ancientsites.com/ aw/Thread/365722.

2 Pfeffer, Jeffrey, *Managing with Power: Politics and Influence in Organizations* (Boston, MA: Harvard Business School Press, 1992).

3 Arrian, *Arrian: The Campaigns of Alexander,* translated by Aubrey de Sélincourt, notes by J.R. Hamilton (London: Penguin Books, 1958 & 1971), 362-363.

4 French, J.R.P., and B. H. Rave, *The basis of social power.* Eds. D. Cartwright, and A. Zander, Group Dynamics, 3rd ed., (New York: Harper & Row, 1968).

5 Nahavandi, Afsaneh, *The Art and Science of Leadership* (Upper Saddle River, NJ: Prentice-Hall, Inc., 1997), 77-79.

6 Yukl, G. and C. M. Falbe, *The Importance of Different Power Sources in Downward and Lateral Relations* (Journal of Applied Psychology, 1991), 76, 416-423.

7 BrainyMedia, "Martin Luther King Quotes," http://www.brainyquote.com/quotes/quotes/m/martinluth166528.html.

8 Bennis, Warren, and Burt Nanus, *Leaders: Strategies for Taking Charge* (New York: HarperCollins Publishers, 1997), 85.

9 Arrian, Aubrey de Sélincourt, and J. R. Hamilton, *Arrian: The Campaigns of Alexander* (London: Penguin Books, 1958 & 1971), 112.

10 Public Domain Image, "Battle of Issus," http://en.wikipedia.org/wiki/Image: Battle_of_Issus.jpg.

11 Nahavandi, Afsaneh, *The Art and Science of Leadership* (Upper Saddle River, NJ: Prentice-Hall, Inc., 1997), 186.

12 Smith, Perry M., *Rules and Tools for Leaders: How to Run an Organization Successfully* (New York: Avery Publishing Group, 1998), 3.

13 The History Channel, *The True Story of Alexander the Great*, A&E Television Networks, 2005.

14 BrainyMedia, "Karl von Clausewitz Quotes," http://www.brainyquote.com/quotes/quotes/k/karlvoncla142329.html.

15 BrainyMedia, "Martin Luther King Quotes," http:/www.
   brainyquote.com/quotes/quotes/m/martinluth101378.
   html.

16 Rufus, Quintus Curtius, *The History of Alexander,* translated
   by John Yardley, introduction and notes by Waldemar
   Heckel (London: Penguin Books, 1984), 225-6.

17 Nahavandi, Afsaneh, *The Art and Science of Leadership* (Upper
   Saddle River, NJ: Prentice-Hall, Inc., 1997).

18 BrainyMedia, "Napoleon Bonaparte Quotes," http://www.
   brainyquote.com/quotes/quotes/n/napoleonbo106371.
   html.

19 Rufus, Quintus Curtius, *The History of Alexander,* translated
   by John Yardley, introduction and notes by Waldemar
   Heckel (London: Penguin Books, 1984), 81.

20 Bennis, Warren, and Burt Nanus, *Leaders: Strategies for Taking
   Charge* (New York: HarperCollins Publishers, 1997), xiii.

NOTES TO CHAPTER VII

1 Reynolds, Siimon, *Thoughts of Chairman Buffett* (New York:
   HarperCollins, 1998).

2 Nahavandi, Afsaneh, *The Art and Science of Leadership* (Upper
   Saddle River, NJ: Prentice-Hall, Inc., 1997), 188.

3 Thomas Nelson, Inc., *The Holy Bible, New King James Version,*
   (National Publishing Company, 1985, 1983), Proverbs 22:1.

4 Rufus, Quintus Curtius, *The History of Alexander,* translated
   by John Yardley, introduction and notes by Waldemar
   Heckel (London: Penguin Books, 1984), 195.

5 Pfeffer, Jeffrey, *Managing with Power: Politics and Influence in Organizations* (Boston, MA: Harvard Business School Press, 1992), 142.

6 Mnzkabinett, "Head of Alexander the Great," http://www.biblepicturegallery.com/free/Pics/Alexand1.gif.

7 Arrian, Aubrey de Sélincourt, and J.R. Hamilton, *Arrian: The Campaigns of Alexander* (London: Penguin Books, 1958 & 1971), 70-71.

8 Caratini, Roger, *Alejandro Magno,* translated by Mauro Armiño (Barcelona, Spain: Plaza & Janes Editores, S.A., 1995 & 2000), 145.

9 Murray, Alan, *A Tale of Two CEOs: How Public Perception Shapes Reputations* (New York: Dow Jones & Company, Inc., The Wall Street Journal, 2006), A2.

10 Murray, Alan, *A Tale of Two CEOs: How Public Perception Shapes Reputations* (New York: Dow Jones & Company, Inc., The Wall Street Journal, 2006), A2.

NOTES TO CHAPTER VIII

1 Rufus, Quintus Curtius, *The History of Alexander,* translated by John Yardley, introduction and notes by Waldemar Heckel (London: Penguin Books, 1984), 194.

2 Bennis, Warren, and Burt Nanus, *Leaders: Strategies for Taking Charge* (New York: HarperCollins Publishers, 1997), 73.

3 Diodorus, *Diodorus of Sicily, The Library of History, Books XVI.66-XVII,* Translated by C. Bradford Welles (Cambridge, Massachusetts: Harvard University Press, Loeb Classical Library, 2003), 423.

4 Rufus, Quintus Curtius, *The History of Alexander,* translated by John Yardley, introduction and notes by Waldemar Heckel (London: Penguin Books, 1984), 194.

5 BrainyMedia, "Plutarch Quotes," http://www.brainyquote.com/quotes/quotes/p/plutarch159950.html.

6 Rufus, Quintus Curtius, *The History of Alexander,* translated by John Yardley, introduction and notes by Waldemar Heckel (London: Penguin Books, 1984), 194.

7 Rufus, Quintus Curtius, *The History of Alexander,* translated by John Yardley, introduction and notes by Waldemar Heckel (London: Penguin Books, 1984), 75.

8 Rufus, Quintus Curtius, *The History of Alexander,* translated by John Yardley, introduction and notes by Waldemar Heckel (London: Penguin Books, 1984), 97.

9 Arrian, Aubrey de Sélincourt, and J.R. Hamilton, *Arrian: The Campaigns of Alexander* (London: Penguin Books, 1958 & 1971), 281.

NOTES TO CHAPTER IX

1 BrainyMedia, "Andrew Carnegie Quotes," http://www.brainyquote.com/quotes/authors/a/andrew_carnegie.html.

2 Reynolds, Siimon, *Thoughts of Chairman Buffett* (New York: HarperCollins, 1998).

3 Collins, James, *Good to Great: Why Some Companies Make the Leap ...and Others Don't* (New York: HarperCollins Publishers, 2001).

4 Collins, James, *Good to Great: Why Some Companies Make the Leap ...and Others Don't* (New York: HarperCollins Publishers, 2001), 49.

5 BrainyMedia, "George S. Patton Quotes," http://www.brainyquote.com/quotes/quotes/g/georgespa159766.html.

6 Covey, Stephen R., *The Seven Habits of Highly Effective People: Restoring the Character Ethic* (New York: Fireside, 1990), 51.

7 Newsweek, "Tiger Relies on 'The Brothers' to Ground Him and Help Him Cope With Fame," http://www.newsweek.msnbc.com.

8 Arrian, Aubrey de Sélincourt, and J.R. Hamilton, *Arrian: The Campaigns of Alexander* (London: Penguin Books, 1958 & 1971), 112.

9 Rufus, Quintus Curtius, *The History of Alexander,* translated by John Yardley, introduction and notes by Waldemar Heckel (London: Penguin Books, 1984), 29.

10 Maxwell, John C., *Relationships 101: What Every Leader Needs to Know.* (Nashville, Tennessee: Thomas Nelson, Inc., 2003), 56.

11 Reynolds, Siimon, *Thoughts of Chairman Buffett* (New York: HarperCollins, 1998).

12 Rufus, Quintus Curtius, *The History of Alexander,* translated by John Yardley, introduction and notes by Waldemar Heckel (London: Penguin Books, 1984), 157-158.

NOTES TO CHAPTER X

1 Porter, Michael E., *What is Strategy?* (Boston, MA: Harvard Business Review, November-December, 1996), 77.

2 Pietersen, Willie, *Intelligent Adaptation: Strategy for a Dynamic World* (New York: Columbia ideas at work, Columbia Business School, summer 2006), 2.

3 Merriam-Webster, *Collegiate Dictionary, 11th Edition & Thesaurus* (Electronic Edition on CD-ROM, 2003).

4 Greenwald, Bruce and Judd Kahn, *Competition Demystified* (New York: Columbia ideas at work, Columbia Business School, summer 2006), 6.

5 Greenwald, Bruce and Judd Kahn, *Competition Demystified: A Radically Simplified Approach to Business Strategy* (New York: Portfolio, 2005).

6 BrainyMedia, "Louis Pasteur Quotes," http://www.brainyquote. com/quotes/authors/l/louis_pasteur.html.

7 Art Branch Inc., "The Art of War - Chapter 4. Tactical Disposition," http://www. literaturecollection.com/a/sun_ tzu/artofwar/11/.

8 BrainyMedia, "Napoleon Bonaparte Quotes," http://www. brainyquote.com/quotes/quotes/n/napoleonbo166656. html.

9 Arrian, Aubrey de Sélincourt, and J.R. Hamilton, *Arrian: The Campaigns of Alexander* (London: Penguin Books, 1958 & 1971), 131-132.

10 Arrian, Aubrey de Sélincourt, and J.R. Hamilton, *Arrian: The Campaigns of Alexander* (London: Penguin Books, 1958 & 1971), 132.

11 BrainyMedia, "Edward de Bono Quotes," http://www. brainyquote.com.

12 Drucker, Peter F, *What Makes and Effective Executive* (Boston, MA: Harvard Business Review, June 2004), 5.

13 Auletta, Ken, "A Conversation with Ted Turner," http://www. kenauletta.com/2003_03_18_tedturner.html.

NOTES TO CHAPTER XI

1 BrainyMedia, "Karl von Clausewitz Quotes," http://www. brainyquote.com.

NOTES TO CHAPTER XII

1 BrainyMedia, "Sun Tzu Quotes," http://www.brainyquote.com.

2 Fisher, R., W. Ury, and B. Patton, *Getting to Yes: Negotiating Agreement without Giving In.* (New York: Penguin, 1991).

3 Graham, John L., *Brazilian, Japanese and American Business Negotiations* (Journal of International Business Studies, 1983) 14, 47-61.

4 Morris, Michael and Paul Ingram, *Trust and Reciprocity in American and Chinese Business Networks* (New York: Columbia Ideas at Work, Columbia Business School, winter 2006), 2.

5 Lewicki, Roy J., David M. Saunders, and John W. Minton, *Essentials of Negotiation* (New York: McGraw-Hill, 2001).

6 Arrian, Aubrey de Sélincourt, and J.R. Hamilton, *Arrian: The Campaigns of Alexander* (London: Penguin Books, 1958 & 1971), 128.

7 Arrian, Aubrey de Sélincourt, and J. R. Hamilton, *Arrian: The Campaigns of Alexander* (London: Penguin Books, 1958 & 1971), 144.

8 Lewicki, Roy J., David M. Saunders, and John W. Minton, *Essentials of Negotiation.* (New York: McGraw-Hill, 2001).

NOTES TO CHAPTER XIII

1 BrainyMedia, "Thomas A. Edison Quotes," http://www.brainyquote.com.

2 BrainyMedia, "Calvin Coolidge Quotes," http://www.brainyquote.com.

3 BrainyMedia, "Thomas Jefferson Quotes," http://www.brainyquote.com.

4 BrainyMedia, "Theodore Roosevelt Quotes," http://www.brainyquote.com.

5 BrainyMedia, "John Quincy Adams Quotes," http://www.brainyquote.com.

6 The History Channel, *The True Story of Alexander the Great*, A&E Television Networks, 2005.

7 BrainyMedia, "Wayne Gretzky Quotes," http://www.brainyquote.com.

8 BrainyMedia, "Henry A. Kissinger Quotes," http://www.brainyquote.com.

9 Porter, Michael E., *What is Strategy?* (Boston, MA: Harvard Business Review, November-December, 1996), 70.

10 BrainyMedia, "Napoleon Bonaparte Quotes,"http://www. brainyquote.com/quotes/quotes/n/napoleonbo124809.html.

11 Rufus, Quintus Curtius, *The History of Alexander,* translated by John Yardley, introduction and notes by Waldemar Heckel (London: Penguin Books, 1984), 122.

12 Rufus, Quintus Curtius, *The History of Alexander,* translated by John Yardley, introduction and notes by Waldemar Heckel (London: Penguin Books, 1984), 122.

13 Rufus, Quintus Curtius, *The History of Alexander,* translated by John Yardley, introduction and notes by Waldemar Heckel (London: Penguin Books, 1984), 122.

14 Rufus, Quintus Curtius, *The History of Alexander,* translated by John Yardley, introduction and notes by Waldemar Heckel (London: Penguin Books, 1984), 168-9.

NOTES TO CHAPTER XIV

1 BrainyMedia, "Nikita Khrushchev Quotes," http://www. brainyquote.com.

2 French, J.R.P., and B.H. Rave, *Group Dynamics* (New York: Harper & Row, 1968).

3 Nahavandi, Afsaneh, *The Art and Science of Leadership* (Upper Saddle River, NJ: Prentice-Hall, Inc., 1997), 77-79.

4 Yukl, G. and Falbe, C.M., *The importance of different power sources in downward and lateral relations* (Journal of Applied Psychology, 1991).

5 BrainyMedia, "George Eliot Quotes," http://www.brainyquote.com.

6 Nelson, Thomas, Inc, *The Holy Bible, New King James Version* (National Publishing Company, 1982).

7 Hope, Jeremy, and Robin Fraser, *New Ways of Setting Rewards: The Beyond Budgeting Model* (California Management Review, University of California, Berkeley, Haas School of Business, winter 2003), 118.

8 Nahavandi, Afsaneh, *The Art and Science of Leadership* (Upper Saddle River, NJ: Prentice-Hall, Inc., 1997), 78.

9 BrainyMedia, "Napoleon Bonaparte Quotes," http://www.brainyquote.com/quotes/quotes/n/napoleonbo108867.html

10 Rufus, Quintus Curtius, *The History of Alexander,* translated by John Yardley, introduction and notes by Waldemar Heckel (London: Penguin Books, 1984), 161.

NOTES TO CHAPTER XV

1 Collins, James, and Jerry Porras, *Built to Last* (New York: HarperCollins Publishers), 91.

2 Porter, Michael E., *What is Strategy?* (Boston, MA: Harvard Business Review, November-December, 1996), 77.

3 BrainyMedia, "Napoleon Bonaparte Quotes," http://www.brainyquote.com/quotes/quotes/n/napoleonbo161724.html.

4 The Quotations Page, "Quotation Details," http://www.quotationspage.com/quote/26595.html.

5 BrainyMedia, "Jack Welch Quotes," http://www.brainyquote.
com/quotes/quotes/j/jackwelch110363.html.

6 BrainyMedia, "John F. Kennedy Quotes," http://www.
brainyquote.com/quotes/quotes/j/johnfkenn121068.
html.

7 Plutarch, John Dryden, Arthur Hugh Clough and Victor Davis
Hanson, *The Life of Alexander the Great* (New York: The
Modern Library, 1992 & 2004), 9.

8 Pfeffer, Jeffrey, *Managing with Power: Politics and Influence in
Organizations* (Boston, MA: Harvard Business School
Press, 1992), 247.

9 BrainyMedia, "Larry King Quotes," http://www.brainyquote.
com/quotes/quotes/l/larryking106582.html.

10 BrainyMedia, "Thomas Jefferson Quotes," http://www.
brainyquote.com/quotes/quotes/t/thomasjeff103570.
html.

11 Inspire21.com http://www.inspire21.com/1RMC/selection2.
html.

12 BrainyMedia, "Bret Harte Quotes," http://www.brainyquote.
com/quotes/quotes/b/bretharte106576.html.

NOTES TO CHAPTER XVI

1 BrainyMedia, "James Madison Quotes," http://www.
brainyquote.com/quotes/quotes/j/jamesmadis122668.
html.

2 BrainyMedia, "William J. Clinton Quotes," http://www.
brainyquote.com/quotes/quotes/w/williamjc148141.html.

3 Rufus, Quintus Curtius, *The History of Alexander*, translated by John Yardley, introduction and notes by Waldemar Heckel (London: Penguin Books, 1984), 218.

4 BrainyMedia, "George Soros Quotes," http://www.brainyquote.com/quotes/quotes/g/georgesoro127398.html.

5 AfterQuotes, "David Packard Quotations," http://www.afterquotes.com/great/people/david-packard/index.htm.

6 Drucker, Peter F, *What Makes and Effective Executive* (Boston, MA: Harvard Business Review, June 2004).

NOTES TO CHAPTER XVII

1 BrainyMedia, "Alexander The Great Quotes," http://www.brainyquote.com/quotes/quotes/a/alexandert148611.html.

2 The History Channel, *The True Story of Alexander the Great*, A&E Television Networks, 2005.

3 Rufus, Quintus Curtius, *The History of Alexander*, translated by John Yardley, introduction and notes by Waldemar Heckel (London: Penguin Books, 1984), 83.

4 Castaigne, Andre, Image in Public Domain, "The Charge of the Persian Scythed Chariots at the Battle of Gaugamela," (1898, 1899), http://en.wikipedia.org/wiki/Image:The_charge_of_the_Persian_scythed_chariots_at_the_battle_of_Gaugamela_by_Andre_Castaigne_%281898-1899%29.jpg.

5 Rufus, Quintus Curtius, *The History of Alexander*, translated by John Yardley, introduction and notes by Waldemar Heckel (London: Penguin Books, 1984), 195.

6 Rufus, Quintus Curtius, *The History of Alexander*, translated by John Yardley, introduction and notes by Waldemar Heckel (London: Penguin Books, 1984), 218.

7 The History Channel, *The True Story of Alexander the Great*, A&E Television Networks, 2005.

8 Public Domain Image, "The Death of Alexander the Great after the painting by Karl von Piloty (1886)," http://commons.wikimedia.org/wiki/Image:The_Death_of_Alexander_the_Great_after_the_painting_by_Karl_von_Piloty_(1886).jpg.

9 BrainyMedia, "George Eliot Quotes," http://www.brainyquote.com.

10 Yukl, G. and C. M. Falbe, *The Importance of Different Power Sources in Downward and Lateral relations* (Journal of Applied Psychology, 1991), 76, 416-423.

11 BrainyMedia, "Napoleon Bonaparte Quotes," http://www.brainyquote.com/quotes/quotes/n/napoleonbo124809.html.

12 Rufus, Quintus Curtius, *The History of Alexander*, translated by John Yardley, introduction and notes by Waldemar Heckel (London: Penguin Books, 1984), 194.

13 BrainyMedia, "Aristotle Quotes," http://www.brainyquote.com/quotes/quotes/a/aristotle145967.html.

14 Arrian, *Arrian: The Campaigns of Alexander,* translated by
    Aubrey de Sélincourt, notes by J. R. Hamilton (London:
    Penguin Books, 1958 & 1971), 294.

NOTES TO MAP

1 Botsford, George Willis, Image in Public Domain, *A History of
    the Ancient World,* (New York: The MacMillan Company,
    1913).

AncientWorlds LLC. http://www.ancientsites.com.

Arrian. *Arrian: The Campaigns of Alexander.* Translated by Aubrey
de Sélincourt, notes by J. R. Hamilton. London: Penguin
Books, 1958 & 1971.

Art Branch Inc. "The Art of War - Chapter 4. Tactical Disposition." http://www.literaturecollection.com/a/sun_tzu/
artofwar/11/.

Auletta, Ken. "A Conversation with Ted Turner." http://www.
kenauletta.com/2003_03_18_tedturner.html.

Bennis, Warren, and Burt Nanus. *Leaders: Strategies for Taking
Charge.* New York: HarperCollins Publishers, 1997.

Botsford, George Willis. *A History of the Ancient World.* New York:
The MacMillan Company, 1913.

BrainyMedia.com. "BrainyQuote." http://www.brainyquote.com.

Brown, Eric. *Plato: Ethics and Politics in the Republic.* Stanford En-
cyclopedia of Philosophy, 2003.

Brown University. Division of Engineering. http://www.engin.
brown.edu.

Caratini, Roger. *Alejandro Magno.* Translated by Mauro Armiño.
Barcelona, Spain: Plaza & Janes Editores, S.A., 1995 &
2000.

Collins, James. *Good to Great: why some companies make the leap
...and others don't.* New York: HarperCollins Publishers,
2001.

Collins, James, and Jerry Porras. *Built to Last.* New York: Harper-Collins Publishers, 2002.

Covey, Stephen R. *The Seven Habits of Highly Effective People: Restoring the Character Ethic.* New York: Fireside, 1990.

Diodorus. *Diodorus of Sicily, The Library of History, Books XVI.66-XVII.* Translated by C. Bradford Welles. Cambridge, Massachusetts: Harvard University Press, Loeb Classical Library, 2003.

Drucker, Peter F. *What Makes and Effective Executive.* Boston, MA: Harvard Business Review, June 2004.

Fisher, R., W. Ury, and B. Patton. *Getting to Yes: Negotiating Agreement without Giving In.* New York: Penguin, 1991.

French, J.R.P., and B. H. Rave. *The Basis of Social Power.* Edited by D. Cartwright and A. Zander. Group Dynamics. 3rd edition. New York: Harper & Row, 1968.

Fox, Robin Lane. *Alexander the Great.* London: Penguin Books, 1986.

Gabriel, Richard A. and Karen S. Metz. *A Short History of War: The Evolution of Warfare and Weapons.* Strategic Studies Institute, U.S. Army War College, 1992. http://www.au.af.mil/au/awc/awcgate/gabrmetz/gabr0000.htm.

Gardner, John W. *On Leadership.* New York: Free Press, 1990.

Graham, J. L. *Brazilian, Japanese and American Business Negotiations.* Journal of International Business Studies, 1983.

Greenwald, Bruce, and Judd Kahn. *Competition Demystified.* New York: Columbia Ideas at Work, Columbia Business School, summer 2006.

Greenwald, Bruce, and Judd Kahn. *Competition Demystified: A Radically Simplified Approach to Business Strategy.* New York: Portfolio, 2005.

Hope, Jeremy, and Robin Fraser. *New Ways of Setting Rewards: The Beyond Budgeting Model.* California Management Review, University of California, Berkeley: Haas School of Business, winter 2003.

Inspire21.com. http://www.inspire21.com.

Koegel, Timothy J. *The Exceptional Presenter.* Washington, DC: The Koegel Group, 2002.

Lewicki, Roy J., David M. Saunders, and John W. Minton. *Essentials of Negotiation.* New York: McGraw-Hill, 2001.

Maxwell, John C. *Relationships 101: What Every Leader Needs to Know.* Nashville, Tennessee: Thomas Nelson, Inc., 2003.

Merriam-Webster. *Collegiate Dictionary, 11th Edition & Thesaurus.* Electronic Edition on CD-ROM, 2003.

Morris, Michael, and Paul Ingram. *Trust and Reciprocity in American and Chinese Business Networks.* New York: Columbia Ideas at Work, Columbia Business School, winter 2006.

Murray, Alan. *A Tale of Two CEOs: How Public Perception Shapes Reputations.* New York: Dow Jones & Company, Inc., The Wall Street Journal, 2006.

Nahavandi, Afsaneh. *The Art and Science of Leadership.* Upper Saddle River, NJ: Prentice-Hall, Inc., 1997.

Nelson, Thomas, Inc. *The Holy Bible, New King James Version.* National Publishing Company, 1982.

Newsweek. "Tiger Relies on 'The Brothers' to Ground Him and Help Him Cope With Fame." http://www.newsweek.msnbc.com.

Pietersen, Willie. *Intelligent Adaptation: Strategy for a Dynamic World*. New York: Columbia Ideas at Work, Columbia Business School, summer 2006.

Pfeffer, Jeffrey. *Managing with Power: Politics and Influence in Organizations*. Boston, MA: Harvard Business School Press.

Plutarch, John Dryden, Arthur Hugh Clough, and Victor Davis Hanson. *The Life of Alexander the Great*. New York: The Modern Library, 1992 & 2004.

Porter, Michael E. *What is Strategy?* Boston, MA: Harvard Business Review, November-December, 1996.

Reynolds, Siimon. *Thoughts of Chairman Buffett*. New York: HarperCollins, 1998.

Rufus, Quintus Curtius. *The History of Alexander*. Translated by John Yardley, introduction and notes by Waldemar Heckel. London: Penguin Books, 1984.

Smith, Perry M. *Rules and Tools for Leaders: How to Run an Organization Successfully*. New York: Avery Publishing Group, 1998.

The History Channel. *Julius Caesar's Rome*. A&E Television Networks, 2005.

The History Channel. *The True Story of Alexander the Great*. A&E Television Networks, 2005.

Thomas Nelson, Inc. *The Holy Bible, New King James Version*. Nashville, TN: National Publishing Company, 1985, 1983.

Wheeler, Benjamin Ide. *Alexander the Great: The Merging of East and West in Universal History.* New York and London: G.P. Putnam's Sons, 1900.

Yukl, G., and C. M. Falbe. *The Importance of Different Power Sources in Downward and Lateral Relations.* Journal of Applied Psychology, 1991.

Made in the USA
Monee, IL
27 January 2021